T0293325

Creating the Organization of the Future

Creating the Organization of the Future: Building on Drucker and Confucius Foundations

BERNARD JAWORSKI

Claremont Graduate University, USA

And

VIRGINIA CHEUNG

Shenzhen University, China

United Kingdom – North America – Japan – India – Malaysia – China

Emerald Publishing Limited
Howard House, Wagon Lane, Bingley BD16 1WA, UK

First published as 当德鲁克遇见孔夫子 ("*Setting the Direction for Your Firm*") by Orient Publishing Center ("OPC"), with Bernard Jaworski and Virginia Cheung, China, 2021. English language translation copyright © 2023, Emerald Publishing Limited. This English language edition published under exclusive licence from OPC by Emerald Publishing Limited.
Translated by Bernard Jaworski and Virginia Cheung.
The moral right of the copyright holder and translator has been asserted.

Reprints and permissions service
Contact: permissions@emeraldinsight.com

British Library Cataloguing in Publication Data
A catalogue record for this book is available from the British Library

ISBN: 978-1-83753-217-9 (Print)
ISBN: 978-1-83753-216-2 (Online)
ISBN: 978-1-83753-218-6 (Epub)

INVESTOR IN PEOPLE

Table of Contents

List of Figures and Tables

About the Authors

Bernard Jaworski is the Drucker Chair in Management and the Liberal Arts, which is named in honor of Peter Drucker, the founder of modern management and the namesake of the Drucker School. Bernard is a ISBM and AMA Marketing Fellow. He is the recipient of the three major *Journal of Marketing* awards – the Alpha Kappa Psi award (received twice), the Maynard award, and the Sheth award. He also received the Converse award and Vijay Mahajan lifetime achievement award for contributions to marketing. His 2020 book on Organic Growth (with Bob Lurie) received the Leonard Berry AMA book of the year award. His work is highly cited (over 49,000 citations as of March 2022). He has been voted MBA teacher of the year (both at USC and Drucker).

Jaworski comes to the Drucker School from the Switzerland-based IMD, a highly regarded international business school. Prior to working at IMD, Jaworski spent a decade as a senior partner of the Monitor Group, a global management consulting firm. During his Monitor career, he cofounded and coled two of the global practice areas, the e-commerce practice and the executive education unit. Among other activities, he was a senior team member of a number of significant multiyear corporate transformations for multinational clients in a variety of sectors, notably pharmaceuticals, biotech, and medical devices.

From 1996 to 1999, Jaworski served as the Jeanne and David Tappan Marketing Fellow and a tenured full professor of Marketing at the University of Southern California. He has also served on the faculty at the University of Arizona and as a visiting professor at Harvard Business School as well as on the review boards of the *Journal of Marketing* and the *Journal of Marketing Research*. He is the coauthor four textbooks on e-commerce and has taught topics including leadership, corporate strategy, and service management.

Virginia Cheung is Associate Research Fellow at the School of Management, Shenzhen University. She holds a PhD in Management from the Peter F. Drucker and Masatoshi Ito Management School at Claremont Graduate University. Her research interests span the integration of both Western and Eastern thought leadership as it relates to leadership, management, and a functioning society. Virginia is interested in comparative research on alternative management philosophies and approaches, with a specific subinterest in how these philosophies are approached in different cultures. Her research focused on the relationship between Drucker philosophy and Confucianism.

Prior to her PhD, Virginia had extensive industry experience in the Greater China region and Germany. Virginia is former director of business development and deputy director of capital market of Phoenix Satellite Television, a leading Chinese omni-media group. She held positions of strategic planner and analyst in Siemens AG in Germany, one of the largest multinational conglomerate manufacturing companies in Europe. She serves and has served on the boards of two big data starts-ups in China and held an adjunct professor title in Beijing Jiaotong University, a prominent university in regard to transportation science and technology.

Virginia also holds an EMBA from the Drucker School, a Master in Law and Economics (LLM) from the University of Hamburg in Germany, and an undergraduate degree in Economics from the University of Bradford in the United Kingdom.

Preface

Our experience is that most organizations start with a product or service idea. In the case of a product or software, the engineers go to work to craft a better solution than exists in the marketplace. The same is true of service businesses. The aim is to provide a product or service that is regarded by the market as much better than competing offers. If successful, the product or service gets adopted by lead users, and over time the organization gains customers, adds employees, and experiences revenue growth. If all goes well, it grows from a small start-up to a healthy mid-size or large firm.

At this stage, we observe that organizations take one of two paths. The first is positive. The firm continues to renew itself. It closely monitors marketplace developments and can meet current marketplace needs as well as transition to the future marketplace. Thus, it balances competing in two time periods, the current marketplace and the future marketplace. This is what Peter Drucker termed "managing continuity and change." For a variety of reasons, this is very hard to do. But a select few firms can and do make this happen. The second pathway is quite the opposite. The firm "locks" in on a business model, optimizes the business model, and, as a result, is unable to reinvent itself to compete in the future. Kodak, Blackberry, and Nokia are all examples of firms that competed well in a particular historical period but were not able to pivot to a new business model. Unfortunately, many firms follow this second path.

There are many reasons why this pivot does not happen. One critical reason is that the senior leadership remains technology- or product-focused rather than asking the basic question of "what business are we in?" Kodak was not in the business of cameras and film: It was in the business of creating memories. The technology to make memories is constantly evolving, but recording these events will ensure that they are with us forever.

Five Content Domains

If one is satisfied with just competing with a core product in one historical time period, then it may not be necessary to set the direction for the firm. However, if the organization aims to be around for a long period of time, it is essential to address all five domains covered in this book. Collectively, these answers provide both the collective goal for the firm that transcends a particular historical period as well as the values and culture to achieve the target. In the best of all worlds the direction-setting activities place the firm on a course not just to respond to marketplace developments but also to shape the evolution of the market. As Drucker often reminded us, great executives do not simply adapt to changing market conditions; rather, they influence the economic conditions in which the firm competes. In particular, this involves five key areas:

- The mission enables the firm to go beyond the "offering" to focus on the core customer benefit. The core customer benefit in Kodak's case – memories – lasts for decades if not centuries. It is not bound to one historical period.
- The vision articulates the fundamental target or goal for the enterprise. What does the world look like when you have accomplished your mission? Often this vision takes decades to achieve: It is ambitious, motivating, and energizes the workforce.
- The purpose of an organization answers a simple question, "why do we exist?" At the most fundamental level, how does your community or society benefit from the presence of your organization? Why do you make the world a better place? A strong purpose is rooted in ways that organizations help society function.
- The values of the organization provide the guardrails for ideal behavior in the firm. How are we going to go about achieving our mission and vision? What is the right set of beliefs and behaviors to guide all employees?
- And, finally, culture is how the work currently gets done inside the firm. What are the rituals, norms, and beliefs that shape how work gets done now? What type of culture does the firm want to put in place to compete now and in the future?

These five domains can be divided into two major parts: one that is externally focused on the marketplace (mission, vision, purpose) and one internally focused on how the work gets done inside the firm (values and culture). The mission and the vision are typically focused on your served market. The mission answers the question "what business are we in?" and the vision is focused on the achievement of that mission (i.e., what is the specific goal that we achieve if we accomplish our mission?). Finally, the purpose is rooted in the marketplace, but it goes beyond the customer. Instead, it is focused on the broader community or societal impact of your mission and vision. The key question, "why do we exist?" must be answered from a societal perspective.

In sharp contrast, the remaining two domains of direction setting – values and culture – focus on how the work gets done within the organization. What are the ways we want our organization to ideally operate (i.e., our values) and how can our culture support our vision? In general, the setting of values and culture should come after the establishing of a mission, vision, and purpose. The rationale is that different missions and visions require different cultures. A mission that is focused on "convenience and easy access" requires a very different culture than one focused on "the best cutting-edge technology." The former may emphasize a customer-service-driven culture while a technology orientation may mean focusing on a culture of technology innovation.

Finally, the strategy of the firm – the specific, integrated set of choices related to "where to play" and "how do we win" in an industry – must follow from setting the direction. Strategy should be articulated in the context of a clear mission, vision, and purpose. Without a clear mission and vision, the senior leadership team has no context to make choices around markets to serve (or not serve) the specific positioning of the organization or the capabilities that need to be built to support their position.

Structure of This Book

This book is organized into two broad sections. The first section focuses on how to build a compelling mission, vision, purpose, culture, and vision. Each of these chapters follows a similar structure by identifying the key criteria to judge the quality of the concept, providing a few examples of the concept and then providing some guidance on how to do it. The aim here is for readers to be able to create or critique their existing mission, vision, purpose, values, and culture (MVPVC). This first section concludes with two chapters (Chapters 6 and 7) that provide guidance on how to "get started" on the journey.

The second section of the book (i.e., Chapters 8–10) focuses on the ideas of Peter Drucker and Confucianism. Drucker had a view on mission, culture, and values, and these are captured in Chapter 8. At the same time, Confucianism is a human-centered philosophy that operates at the individual, relationship, family, and societal levels. For society to function well, individuals need to engage in acts that put society first and individual self-interests second. As such, our intent in Chapter 8 is to demonstrate the linkages between each author as they relate to mission, vision, purpose, values, and culture. We conclude the second section with an overview of the work of Drucker (Chapter 9) and the writings of Confucianism (Chapter 10). Their collective work is the foundation for Chapters 1 through 5.

Building on Their Work

Importantly, we use the term "foundation" to mean that we are building on their work and moving it forward into the twenty-first century. In particular, we enhance and contemporize their work in five specific ways. First, business practices have advanced. For example, today's business world is highly networked both in terms of "ecosystems" of players that compete against other ecosystems and in terms of the tidal wave of change brought about by digitization. Drucker could not have forecast the fundamental shift in both forms of networks. Furthermore, the emergence of purpose-led organizations and brands has only truly emerged since his death in 2005. Our key point is that the world of business has changed and that we need to update our thinking about this world to reflect this change.

Second, business theory has advanced. Much has been written in the past 20 years that has pushed our knowledge of management forward. For example, Drucker did not have a distinctive position on purpose. Rather, his writing on mission included purpose. Given how much has changed regarding the role of purpose in organizations – we offer the examples of Microsoft, J&J, Unilever, and several others as case studies in Chapter 3 – we believe it is now exceptionally important to craft a stand-alone chapter on purpose. Purpose is distinct from mission, and this must be acknowledged. More generally, the advancement of business theory is reflected *throughout* this book.

Third, we have advanced our own thinking on the topic, and we want to share our perspective. For example, all of the chapters in the first section specify criteria to assess the quality of the concept (e.g., five specific criteria to evaluate a mission statement). This is our perspective, not that of Drucker or Confucianism. We have spent a good deal of time thinking about these issues, and we want to share our viewpoint.

Fourth, we shift from concepts to very practical guidance in Chapters 6 and 7. This is distinct from Drucker since he was focused more on the novel concept than the exact details of crafting the statements. This is not to say whether he would agree with us (or not), but "how do get started on the journey?" would not be part of a typical Drucker book or manuscript.

Fifth, we introduce new concepts and language to enhance the precision of work and reflect the changes that are unfolding in organizations. This is reflected throughout the entire book – in particular, the examples, criteria, and identification of the best-of-class illustrations in the first section. Each of these sections includes new thinking and language that moves practice forward. Our purpose is to use the wonderful thinking of Drucker and Confucius as a platform for building practical and straightforward advice on how to construct your mission, vision, purpose, culture, and values – and, ideally, shape the markets in which you compete. Collectively, these five choices set both the direction of the firm (e.g., purpose, vision, mission) and the ways the work gets done (e.g., culture and values). We hope you enjoy the book and apply the concepts to your firm.

Bernard Jaworski
Claremont, California

Virginia Cheung
Shenzhen, China

Acknowledgments

We would like to thank the many helping hands and minds among our colleagues, clients, family, and friends. Even though there are too many to thank individually, we want to express our deep gratitude to them all here.

We would like to thank Nick Wallwork at Emerald. Nick agreed to our project, sold it inside of Emerald, and guided the book to fruition. We would also like to thank our Chinese editor, Yiting Shen, of Orient Publishing Center. Yiting was the catalyst for a similar set of ideas published for the Chinese market. She encouraged us to pursue an English-language book based on the thinking of Peter Drucker and Confucianism. Finally, Nick Owchar provided expert editorial assistance in reviewing and editing every word of this volume. Thank you, Nick.

We would also like to acknowledge the contributions of Drucker School faculty member Katarina Pick. We worked with Katarina on a "building the organization of the future" project with TCT, a midsize Chinese firm. Here we worked on all five domains that are covered in this volume, and Kat was instrumental in every phase – in particular on the cultural work with the firm. Thank you, Kat: We learned a great deal from you. And special thanks to David Sprott, the dean of the Drucker School, for giving us enormous support to contemporize Drucker's work, helping us to promote the work, and giving us the chance to practice the findings with organizations across the globe.

We also want to mention the contribution of the organizations working with us. We learned a lot from their market sense and vision. Here we would like to single out Chunhai Gao in particular. Mr. Gao applied the principles of Chapters 1–5 within TCT, and their best practices informed our research and ensured the practical value of our research findings. It was a pleasure to work with the organization, and we benefited greatly from this experience.

In addition, we would like to thank the following individuals and colleagues who are a part of our personal networks.

Bernard

I would like to thank my wonderful fiancée Maria. She not only encouraged this effort, she shared the first five chapters with her colleagues at her start-up venture, the Loop Village. The Loop executive team read the chapters and worked through their mission, vision, and values statements. More generally, she has been incredibly supportive of this effort, engaging in countless late-night discussions, encouraging me to put the time aside to write, and showing genuine happiness when I let her know that I'd finished another chapter. Thank you, Maria!

My additional colleagues at the Drucker School also must be acknowledged. I am fortunate to work with an incredible set of supportive faculty colleagues.

I would also like to thank my good friends and colleagues at Capsys, Thrive, and SMA. Almost all are former Monitor colleagues with whom I've had the good fortune of working with over the years. They include David Sanchez, Igor Skender, Frank Blithe, Williams Stephens, Joao Lopes, Eliette Krakora, Ajay Patel, Jacque Keats, and many others.

Virginia

First and foremost, I would like to express my deep and sincere gratitude to my mentor, supervisor, and coauthor Professor Bernard Jaworski. Having the chance to be advised by a top-ranked professor with a global reputation on the research of two major thinkers is a great honor and something I would never have imagined. Professor Jaworski is not only the most authoritative Drucker scholar, he is also a remarkable Drucker practitioner: a living, breathing exemplar of Drucker values and principles, and a true role model for me. The findings we present in this book are based on years of hard research conducted by Professor Jaworski and other brilliant professors of the Drucker School. Professor Jaworski generously shared his profound research findings with me and enlightened me about new research methods. This book would not have been possible without his guidance and vision.

I'm extremely grateful to the Drucker School and to each of the professors there. They are the creators of life-changing magic, and the time I spent at the Drucker School reshaped my mind. My special thanks to Professor Jay Prag, who allowed me to enroll in the PhD program. That was the start of a new chapter in my life. Thank you, Jay, I will remember this forever. Professor Katarina Pick not only taught me useful knowledge, her unique and charming teaching style and her inspiration as a female professor also made a difference in my personal career choice. I'm also grateful to former Drucker School dean Jenny Darroch, who gave me the chance to engage in many school activities. I learned how Drucker principles are practiced in real life through these activities and built a strong attachment to the Drucker School.

I would also like to extend my appreciation to Capsys with special thanks to David Sanchez. David provided invaluable suggestions about how organizations can leverage these findings in order to grow, and I learned a lot from him.

I am very thankful to Yanchun Pan, deputy dean of the School of Management, Shenzhen University, for providing generous support and encouraging me to focus on completing this research work.

Finally, I would like to acknowledge with gratitude the support and love of my family, friends, and partners in China. I can't thank them enough for generously sharing their insights, providing suggestions during the writing process, and promoting the practice of our findings in China. These include Ou Zhang, Zhong Liu, Siyuan Tao, Kim Zhu, Fang Luo, Charles Guo, and many others.

Thank you all for offering me your kind and continuous support.

Chapter 1

Developing an Organization's Mission

Introduction

A well-crafted mission statement may, at first glance, seem rather obvious. Our experience is that it often takes weeks, if not months, for a senior-level team to answer the very basic question, "What business are we in?" Peter Drucker stated the challenge as follows: "Nothing may seem simpler or more obvious than to answer what a company's business is. A steel mill makes steel, a railroad runs trains to carry freight and passengers, an insurance company underwrites fire risks. Indeed, the question looks so simple that it is seldom raised, the answer seems so obvious it is seldom given. Actually, 'what is our business' is almost always a difficult question which can be answered only after hard thinking and study. The answer is usually anything but obvious."[1]

Equally important, the crafting of a mission statement is not simply a nice poster on the wall or a "who we are" message on the website; rather, it is one of the most important decisions of the leadership team. If the mission statement is narrowly focused on current products and technology, the firm will likely miss out on the next generation of products and technology. If it is too broad, it will not help focus the firm's resources: its R&D investments, its people investments, and its selection of target markets. Drucker believed that the business purpose and mission were normally not given sufficient consideration by most firms. He believed that this error was perhaps the *most significant* cause of business frustration and failure.[2]

With these thoughts in mind, mission statements share six basic characteristics. In this chapter, we introduce and discuss these characteristics. As you read this chapter, ask yourself, does my mission statement pass the test for each of these criteria? If not, we strongly advise you to revise your mission statement. We conclude the chapter with a discussion of five mission statements that not only pass the test but represent "best of class" mission statements. We hope you can learn from these case studies.

Creating the Organization of the Future, 1–10

Emerald Publishing Limited, Howard House, Wagon Lane, Bingley BD16 1WA, UK.

First published as 当德鲁克遇见孔夫子 ("*Setting the Direction for Your Firm*") by Orient Publishing Center ("OPC"), with Bernard Jaworski and Virginia Cheung, China, 2021. English language translation copyright © 2023, Emerald Publishing Limited. This English language edition published under exclusive licence from OPC by Emerald Publishing Limited. Translated by Bernard Jaworski and Virginia Cheung. The moral right of the copyright holder and translator has been asserted.

All rights of reproduction in any form reserved

doi:10.1108/978-1-83753-216-220231001

Precise Mission Statements: Getting It Right

Precise mission statements share six basic characteristics: (1) they focus on the core customer benefit, not the existing products or technology; (2) they specify their target customers; (3) they are short—often one sentence; (4) they must fit the theory of the business; (5) they inspire the workforce; and (6) every worker can see how their role can support the mission.

Focus on Underlying Benefits for Customers—Not Products or Technology

Mission statements are customer-centered. They answer the key question, "What is the core customer value that we provide our target market?" They do not articulate current products, offerings, services, or solutions. These product forms are internally focused on what the firm does. Products change, but underlying customer benefits last years if not decades.

Let's take a look at Disney. The mission of The Walt Disney Company is "to entertain, inform and inspire people around the globe through the power of unparalleled storytelling, reflecting the iconic brands, creative minds and innovative technologies that make ours the world's premier entertainment company."[3] There are two parts of this definition that stand out. First, they are in the business of entertainment—their mission is not expressed in terms of movies, theme parks, TV shows, or digital offerings. Yes, these offerings are important—but they do not answer the question of "what business are we in?" Second, across all their properties, the core customer benefit is "storytelling." This is true of their movies, TV programs, and even their theme parks. One can only imagine the length of time it took the senior executive team to arrive at this deeply meaningful benefit that extends across all product lines—currently and in the future.

Specifies the Target Customers

Mission statements must specify your target set of customers. For a company such as Microsoft the target market could be exceptionally broad and for a small startup the core segment could be very narrow. Indeed, one of the major problems with start-ups is that they often spread their resources too thin across many opportunities and segments.

Let's consider Mattel. Their mission is to "create innovative products and experiences that inspire, entertain and develop children through play."[4] Mattel focuses on the children consumer market. Within the mission statement one does not need to provide the details of the target audience (e.g., ages 1–12), but one does need to take a clear position about what portions of the market you do not serve (e.g., Mattel does not focus on the play of teenagers, young adults, or adults). We should also note that, like Disney, Mattel's mission focuses on the core child benefit (i.e., play) and not the core product form (i.e., toys). There was an explicit pivot by the firm several years ago to change their mission from a focus on toys to play.

Keep It Short—One or Two Sentences

Mark Twain once said, "I didn't have time to write you a short letter, so I wrote you a long one instead." In the same spirit, it takes a good amount of time for a senior leadership team to write a one-sentence mission statement. There is a lot to like about IBM's mission statement. The IBM mission statement is "to lead in the creation, development, and manufacture of the industry's most advanced information technologies, including computer systems, software, networking systems, storage devices, and microelectronics. And our worldwide network of IBM solutions and services professionals translates these advanced technologies into business value for our customers. We translate these advanced technologies into value for our customers through our professional solutions, services and consulting businesses worldwide."[5]

While it specifies the underlying customer benefits and their target B2B market, it is very long and wordy. Hence, no employee can remember this statement: It is simply too complex. Moreover, in sharp contrast to our recommendation not to focus on products and technologies, they do focus on current offerings. We would simply shorten it. Our revision would be as follows: "We are a global leader in the creation and development of the world's most advanced information technologies enhancing the productivity and results for our business customers."

Inspirational

Considering both Drucker and Confucianism are human-centered, a precise mission statement should inspire the workforce. Drucker noted that a mission cannot be impersonal; it has to have deep meaning, be something you believe in—something you know is right. Nestle's mission statement "Good Food, Good Life" is captured in a simple slogan and an associated description. "Good Food, Good Life" is "to provide consumers with the best tasting [sic], most nutritious choices in a wide range of food and beverage categories and eating occasions, from morning to night."[6] The key point is that good food supports a good life. Similarly, the mission of Amgen, one of the world's largest biotechnology companies, is to serve patients by transforming the promise of science and biotechnology into therapies that have the power to restore health or save lives.[7] Both of these mission statements are designed to inspire the workforce to deliver on the mission.

Grounded in the Theory of the Business

Recall that a key component of Drucker's thinking is that the mission of the firm must fit the "realities" of the marketplace. He termed this ability to specify the core assumptions of the industry as a key part of his theory of the business. A mission statement must fit comfortably with the key trends, developments, and evolution of the industry. If the core profitability assumptions of the industry change (e.g., the profit in the industry shifts from the product itself to the services or information provided by the product), then the mission must be revisited.

Hence, prior to crafting a mission statement, the senior executive team must agree on the five to eight key trends that are unfolding in the industry and where value is shifting in the industry. This activity should begin with 40–50 trends—and narrow down to the most important. Once these key trends are identified—the executive team must ask "Is our mission still useful, given these trends?" For Mattel, there was a realization that "toys" was a narrow view of play—and industry developments required a shift to the broader benefit of play.

Every Employee Can Contribute to the Mission

As Drucker noted, a fundamental responsibility of leadership is to make sure that everybody knows the mission, understands it, lives it. He stated, "The mission is broad, even eternal, yet directs you to do the right things now and into the future so that everyone in the organization can say, 'What I am doing contributes to the goal.' So, it must be clear, and it must inspire. Every [stakeholder] should be able to see the mission and say, 'Yes. This is something I want to be remembered for.'"[8]

Hence, each employee must ask the question, "What can I do to support the mission of my organization?" What strengths do I possess that enable me to direct my activities and results in support of the mission? This reflection on the "contribution of each individual to the mission" is a conversation each employee should have with his or her boss each year. Interesting this alignment with a broader collective purpose, was consistent with Confucian thinking that individual development is best focused on shared goals rather than individual goals.[9]

If employees cannot see how their role can support the mission statement, the mission statement is not useful—and must be rewritten. Keep in mind: One purpose of the mission statement is to align all employees toward a common goal.

Precise Mission Statements: Examples

Given the six criteria noted above, it is possible to find mission statements that meet all of the criteria. As we noted at the start of the chapter, this is not an easy task—but it is essential for the success of the enterprise.

LinkedIn

> To connect the world's professionals to make them more productive and successful.[10]

LinkedIn has multiple business lines, but they all relate to connecting people. In some cases, the connection is for HR professionals to enhance their recruitment of the right employees. For others, it is about connecting audiences to their LinkedIn learning suite of offerings. Sales professionals also access the LinkedIn network to find, access, and connect with new potential clients. Company revenues come mainly from selling access to its members (e.g., a sales professional can get premium access to the membership to better locate potential target clients). In 2016, the firm was acquired by Microsoft and is now a wholly owned subsidiary. As of December 2021, LinkedIn had over 756 million registered members from over 200 countries and territories.[11]

Let's now turn to the six criteria. The core customer benefit is "connecting" professionals. Why connect? To make the professionals more productive and successful. The target market is the "world's professionals," making the clear distinction between other networking sites that are focused on connecting for a different purpose (e.g., Instagram, Facebook). It is only 12 words—yet it covers its target clients, core benefits, and enables all employees to align against the mission. It fits the underlying shift from face-to-face to "screen to face" connections enabled by the digital world. Finally, it provides direction and inspiration for the workforce, making others successful in their professional role.

Amazon

To be the Earth's most customer-centric company.

In 1995, Amazon's mission statement was to be Earth's most customer-centric company,[12] where customers can find and discover anything they might want to buy online, and to endeavor to offer its customers the lowest possible prices. As of 2021, the mission statement has been shortened to being "the Earth's most customer-centric company." This shift recognizes that Amazon has both its B2C business and its vast B2B business (i.e., Amazon Web Services).

This mission statement is quite unusual and reflects the worldwide dominant position of Amazon. Very few companies in the world could specify such a general statement. What makes this mission statement work is the additional specification of 14 leadership principles, which provide very specific direction and guidance to the entire workforce as noted in Table 1.1.[13] These principles—in combination with the mission statement—inspire and enable the global workforce. These principles are used daily by employees to guide decision-making and resource allocation.

Nike

To bring inspiration and innovation to every athlete in the world.

Nike designs, develops, manufactures, markets, and sells athletic footwear, apparel, equipment, and accessories. It is one of the most valued brands in sports with a market capitalization of $136 billion as of October 2022.[14] It employs nearly 80,000 worldwide and had revenues of over $37 billion.[15]As such, it is 85th in the top 100 of the Fortune 500 firms.[16]

This mission statement focuses on two benefits, inspiration and innovation, which are delivered to their target market (i.e., every athlete in the world). It fits

Table 1.1. Fourteen Amazon Principles.

1	Customer obsession	Leaders start with the customer and work backwards. They work vigorously to earn and keep customer trust. Although leaders pay attention to competitors, they obsess over customers.
2	Ownership	Leaders are owners. They think long-term and don't sacrifice long-term value for short-term results. They act on behalf of the entire company, beyond just their own team. They never say, "That's not my job."
3	Invent and simplify	Leaders expect and require innovation and invention from their teams and always find ways to simplify. They are externally aware, look for new ideas from everywhere, and are not limited by "not invented here." As we do new things, we accept that we may be misunderstood for long periods of time.
4	Are right, a lot	Leaders are right a lot. They have strong judgment and good instincts. They seek diverse perspectives and work to disconfirm their beliefs.
5	Learn and be curious	Leaders are never done learning and always seek to improve themselves. They are curious about new possibilities and act to explore them.
6	Hire and develop the best	Leaders raise the performance bar with every hire and promotion. They recognize exceptional talent, and willingly move them throughout the organization. Leaders develop leaders and take seriously their role in coaching others. We work on behalf of our people to invent mechanisms for development like Career Choice.
7	Insist on the highest standards	Leaders have relentlessly high standards – many people may think these standards are unreasonably high. Leaders are continually raising the bar and drive their teams to deliver high-quality products, services, and processes. Leaders ensure that defects do not get sent down the line and that problems are fixed so they stay fixed.

Table 1.1. *(Continued)*

8 Think big	Thinking small is a self-fulfilling prophecy. Leaders create and communicate a bold direction that inspires results. They think differently and look around corners for ways to serve customers.
9 Bias for action	Speed matters in business. Many decisions and actions are reversible and do not need extensive study. We value calculated risk-taking.
10 Frugality	Accomplish more with less. Constraints breed resourcefulness, self-sufficiency, and invention. There are no extra points for growing headcount, budget size, or fixed expense.
11 Earn trust	Leaders listen attentively, speak candidly, and treat others respectfully. They are vocally self-critical, even when doing so is awkward or embarrassing. Leaders do not believe their or their team's body odor smells of perfume. They benchmark themselves and their teams against the best.
12 Dive deep	Leaders operate at all levels, stay connected to the details, audit frequently, and are skeptical when metrics and anecdotes differ. No task is beneath them.
13 Have backbone; disagree and commit	Leaders are obligated to respectfully challenge decisions when they disagree, even when doing so is uncomfortable or exhausting. Leaders have conviction and are tenacious. They do not compromise for the sake of social cohesion. Once a decision is determined, they commit wholly.
14 Deliver results	Leaders focus on the key inputs for their business and deliver them with the right quality and in a timely fashion. Despite setbacks, they rise to the occasion and never settle.

the evolution of global society trends regarding better health and wellness. It provides enough direction whereby each employee can ask each day "How does my work support the mission?" Finally, it is inspirational insofar that Nike reaches out to the "athlete in all of us."

Amgen

> Amgen strives to serve patients by transforming the promise of science and biotechnology into therapies that have the power to restore health or save lives.

Amgen is one of the world's largest independent biotechnology companies focused on human therapeutics. Its sales revenues for 2020 were $25.4 billion[17] and its market capitalization is over $122 billion.[18] It has over 23,000 employees worldwide.

Amgen's mission to restore health and saves lives is powerful for their target clients (i.e., patients suffering from health conditions) and highly motivating for their workforce. It is precise, empowering, and inspirational. All workers can translate this mission into their work-lives. The scientists at Amgen are focused on breakthrough therapies, the sales force is saving lives by communicating the efficacy of the Amgen therapies, and manufacturing must maintain very high-quality control to grow cell cultures.

Tesla

> To accelerate the world's transition to sustainable energy.[19]

Tesla, as of February 2021, is the world's most valuable automobile manufacturer. With sales of $31 billion,[20] its market capitalization is over $650 billion.[21] This market cap is largely driven by the potential of the electric vehicles to reshape the world's transportation market. Its current products include electric cars, battery energy storage, and solar technology. Tesla's global vehicle sales approached 935,000 units in 2021.

The eight-word mission statement provides an articulation of the core benefit—sustainable energy as well as its approach which is, namely, to accelerate the change. It is an interesting play on words since automobiles also "accelerate" when the gas pedal is pushed. There is a lot to like in this mission statement; it is memorable and believable by the workforce. It can inspire the workforce to accelerate the transition to renewable, sustainable energy.

Assessing Your Mission Statement

It is now your turn to evaluate your current mission statement. Here is your six-question checklist.

(1) Does your mission statement focus on the core benefit(s) that are provided to customers?
(2) Does the statement specify your intended target market?
(3) Is your mission statement one or two sentences that every employee can easily remember and state clearly?
(4) Is your mission statement fully consistent with the underlying trends in your industry and the broader macro environment (e.g., political, social, technology trends)?
(5) Are employees excited, inspired, and energized by your mission?
(6) Can every single employee see how their role and responsibilities support the mission?

If your answer is "no" to any of these questions, your mission statement must be updated. As Drucker noted, this is not any easy and quick fix. The senior management team must reflect deeply on each of these questions. It is often valuable to get input from all levels of the organization. It is also valuable to ask your current customers whether the mission statement is consistent with their view of the firm and the benefits that it delivers. Assume that this crafting process will take time and go through many revisions.

Conclusion

> Defining the purpose and mission of the business is difficult, painful, and risky. But it alone enables a business to set objectives, to develop strategies, to concentrate its resources, and to go to work. It alone enables a business to be managed for performance.[22]

For Drucker, a clear, specific, and inspirational mission statement was a necessary, essential task before setting the strategy and tactics of the firm.

Notes

1. Peter Drucker, *The Practice of Management* (New York: Harper & Row, 1954), 49.
2. Ibid., 50.
3. "Our Mission," The Walt Disney Company, accessed October 8, 2022, https://thewaltdisneycompany.com/about/.
4. "Who We Are," Mattel, accessed October 8, 2022, https://corporate.mattel.com/en-us/about.
5. "IBM (International Business Machines) Mission and Vision Statement Analysis," IBM, accessed October 8, 2022, https://mission-statement.com/ibm/.
6. "Mission & Vision," Nestlé, accessed October 8, 2022, https://www.nestle-esar.com/aboutus/missionvision.

7. "Mission and Values," Amgen, accessed October 8, 2022, https://www.amgen.com/about/mission-and-values.

8. Peter Drucker et al., *The Five Most Important Questions You Will Ever Ask about Your Organization* (San Francisco: John Wiley & Sons, 2011), 14.

9. Confucius, *Book of Rites* and *Great Learning*, http://classics.mit.edu/Confucius/learning.html.

10. "About LinkedIn," LinkedIn, accessed October 8, 2022, https://about.linkedin.com/.

11. Ibid.

12. "14 Core Values of Amazon: Its Mission and Vision Statement," Brandon Gaille, accessed December 7, 2022, https://brandongaille.com/core-values-of-amazon/.

13. "The 14 Leadership Principles that Drive Amazon," *Ian Golding*, July 6, 2017, https://customerthink.com/the-14-leadership-principles-that-drive-amazon/.

14. "Nike Stock Price," Yahoo! Finance, accessed October 8, 2022, https://finance.yahoo.com/quote/NKE/.

15. "Nike's Revenue Worldwide from the Fiscal Years of 2005 to 2022," *Statista*, accessed October 8, 2022, https://www.statista.com/statistics/241683/nikes-sales-worldwide-since-2004/.

16. "Nike on the Fortune 500 Rankings," *Fortune*, accessed October 8, 2022, https://fortune.com/company/nike/fortune500/.

17. "Amgen Reports Fourth Quarter and Full Year 2020 Financial Results," *Cision PR Newswire*, accessed February 2, 2021, https://www.prnewswire.com/news-releases/amgen-reports-fourth-quarter-and-full-year-2020-financial-results-301220622.html.

18. "Amgen Stock Price," Yahoo! Finance, accessed October 8, 2022, https://finance.yahoo.com/quote/AMGN/.

19. "Tesla Mission and Vision Statement Analysis," *Mission-Statement*, accessed October 8, 2022, https://mission-statement.com/tesla/.

20. "Tesla Revenue 2010-2022/TSLA," *Macrotrends*, accessed October 8, 2022, https://www.macrotrends.net/stocks/charts/TSLA/tesla/revenue.

21. Ibid.

22. Peter Drucker, *Post-Capitalist Society* (New York: HarperBusiness, 1994), 94.

Chapter 2

Developing an Organization's Vision

Introduction

A vision statement answers the question, "What does the world look like when we have accomplished our mission?" Since Nike's mission is to bring inspiration and innovation to every athlete in the world, it is important to ask, "What would the world look like if Nike accomplished their mission?" Here Nike has a number of choices. It could focus on the overall number of athlete's impacted by this mission (note: Nike believes that everyone in the world is an athlete) or it could focus on the level of inspiration achieved. Interestingly, Nike's purpose is to move the world forward through the power of sport. With this in mind, the vision could also focus on what it means to "move the world forward." In order words, what metric are we using to measure moving the world forward? Is it the number of people, lives changed by sport, or even the overall physical and mental well-being of the athletes?

Why is it important to specify a vision? Like any key organizational metric, unless we specify a clear objective—or end state—we have no way of charting our progress on our mission. As Drucker noted, clear measures are essential to focus and assess organizational progress. Recall that the World Bank is focused on raising the standard of living for people who are living in extreme poverty. While this is a noble cause in its own right, establishing a clear target makes the mission come to life. The World Bank notes that nearly 800 million people now live in extreme poverty and earn $1.90 per day or less. For the first time, the World Bank has set a deadline for ending extreme poverty by 2030. It is the No. 1 goal of the World Bank Group.

Pepsi's mission is to create more smiles with every sip and bite. To achieve this mission, their vision is to be the global leader in convenient foods and beverages by winning with a purpose. Here their ambition is to win sustainably in the marketplace, accelerate top-line growth and, at the same time, make a commitment to do good for the planet and communities.[1] The end state—being *the* global

Creating the Organization of the Future, 11–19

Emerald Publishing Limited, Howard House, Wagon Lane, Bingley BD16 1WA, UK.

First published as 当德鲁克遇见孔夫子 (*"Setting the Direction for Your Firm"*) by Orient Publishing Center ("OPC"), with Bernard Jaworski and Virginia Cheung, China, 2021. English language translation copyright © 2023, Emerald Publishing Limited. This English language edition published under exclusive licence from OPC by Emerald Publishing Limited. Translated by Bernard Jaworski and Virginia Cheung. The moral right of the copyright holder and translator has been asserted.

All rights of reproduction in any form reserved

doi:10.1108/978-1-83753-216-220231002

leader—is a very clear articulation of their desire to be No. 1. That means beating their major competitor, The Coca-Cola Company.

Why is it challenging to develop a simple vision statement? Often it is difficult to get the organization to commit to a very specific target goal. It is much easier to make a general statement—that, for example, we desire to end poverty or be a "high performing" company. But these generalized statements do not provide the same level of urgency and motivation as does a specific number or target. Performance must be measured for business to perform.[2] Also, a specific target by a specific date means that you publicly commit, and that also means that you can publicly fail to reach the target. As Confucius suggested, evaluation should be based on both words and action.[3] It is fundamental for Confucian virtue of trust to promise only what one can deliver and deliver what has been promised.[4] Finally, the executive leadership team may have very different views of what it means to achieve the mission statement. Collectively, these three forces decrease the chances of developing a clear end state for the organization.

The chapter is organized as follows. We first discuss six characteristics of great vision statements. Next, we introduce five organizations that have crafted clear and specific vision statements. Yet even for some of these five organizations, there is room for improvement. So, we not only identify these well-crafted statements, but we also suggest ways to make them even better. We also provide a list of questions for you to consider as you craft your organization's vision statement.

Great Vision Statements: Getting It Right

Like a mission statement, the vision statement should be simple, clear, and energizing for the workforce. Here we focus attention on six key characteristics of great vision statements: (1) articulates a clear end state, (2) concise, (3) uses image-based language, (4) inspires the workforce, (5) challenging – yet achievable, and (6) distinct from competitors.

Articulates a Clear End State

A vision statement answers the question, "What does the world look like when we are done?" As noted, it is often the case that organizations do not commit to a specific target. Consider SAP, the German multi-national enterprise software firm. Their explicit vision is to "help the world run better and improve people's lives."[5] Not only is the target end state imprecise, but it is also equally unclear what the firm does for a living. Is it an athletic shoe firm? A transportation and logics firm? A healthcare firm?

A similar observation could be made about the world-class accounting and management consulting firm Deloitte. Their vision is to aspire to be the standard of excellence, the first choice of the most sought-after clients and talent. Here we can debate several aspects of this statement. First, while the term "standard of excellence" means the "best," it is not clear what services they deliver: Advice? Consulting? Accounting services? Tax services? All of the above? We do like the more precise term of "first choice" of the most sought-after clients and talent. That, for example, signals a clear "top ranking" of acquiring the best employees in the marketplace. However, "most sought-after" clients are much less precise: Are these the largest firms in the world? The best brands in the world? The best places to work? Or, simply, the most challenging assignments?

Concise—One Sentence

A well-crafted vision statement is one sentence. Marriott International manages over 20 well-known hotel brands—Marriott, the W Hotel, Westin, Sheraton, Ritz-Carlton, Le Meridian—and many others. Its vision statement is quite simple: To be the "World's Favorite Travel Company."[6] The term "favorite" is an excellent choice since it is defined as "preferred before all others of the same kind." Thus, it means to be the top choice among all other competitors in that specific market. So, for the Ritz Carlton it means to be the top choice relative to the Four Seasons and the Mandarin Oriental. For Westin, it means to be favored over Hilton. Thus, while the state is broad, it can be easily translated and applied to each of the divisions.

Image-Based Language

Compared to more abstract language (e.g., our goal is providing a world-class level of customer service in the watch industry), image-based language engages employees' emotion and provides a shared point of reference. Being very clear about the desired long-term outcome reflects the idea that the vision is a clear, specific picture of an ideal future.[7] For a watch company, the clear picture could be as simple as "a watch on every person's arm." It is easy to visualize this statement as compared to a statement that focuses on superior levels of customer service.

Inspires the Workforce

A great vision—much like a great mission—must inspire, motivate, and energize the workforce. In the case of the vision, the target outcome must be one that makes employees proud to be part of the organization. Helping solve world hunger, poverty, or even basic human needs is one that is often inspirational. However, firms in transportation (e.g., safe and reliable, so you can spend more time with your loved ones), technology (e.g., often expressed as some form of faster, better, or less expensive to enhance your productivity), or consumer packaged goods (providing the best quality food while enhancing the sustainability of the planet) can all be crafted in ways that inspire and drive the workforce to achieve as much as possible.

Challenging Yet Achievable

Vision end states are classic "stretch goals." That means that they can be achieved if the organization is highly focused, works hard, and is committed to the task at the end. But these goals are hard to attain. Hence, it requires an unusual level of commitment on the part of the workforce. Thinking about the World Bank's goal to end poverty by 2030 may be unrealistic.

Distinct From Your Competitors

Developing great strategy means developing value propositions that cannot be matched by your competitors. Similarly, one should aim for a distinctive vision statement—not one that your competitors could also comfortably claim. Recall the Deloitte vision to be the standard of excellence, the first choice of the most sought-after clients and talent. This is not a distinctive vision statement since PwC or KPMG could have the exact same statement.

Great Vision Statements: Examples

With the above criteria in mind, it is difficult to find vision statements that pass the test of the entire set of six criteria. Below we discuss six firms that have very strong vision statements. Some are "perfect" as is, and some we make specific suggestions to improve.

IKEA

> Our vision is to create a better everyday life for the many people – for customers, but also for our co-workers and the people who work at our suppliers.[8]

IKEA is a global Swedish conglomerate that designs and sells ready-to-assemble furniture, kitchen appliances and products, and home accessories.[9] As of 2021, IKEA was the most valuable furniture retailer brand in the world, and it is also among the leading retail brands globally. The business operates 445 stores and is present in the world's major markets.[10] IKEA announced retail sales of 35.2 billion euros in the fiscal year to September. That is 1.5 billion less than a year earlier, despite online growth of 60%.[11]

In order to understand what it means to create a better life for many people, it is necessary to understand how they view their core business idea. Here IKEA states that their core business idea is "to offer a wide range of well-designed, functional home furnishing products at prices so low that as many people as possible will be able to afford them." Furthermore, they note that their vision also goes beyond home furnishings. They want to create "a better everyday life" for all people impacted by their business.[12]

There are several aspects of the IKEA vision statement that are notable. It is challenging but clearly achievable. Since it is about improving the lives of individuals across the globe, the statement is inspirational for the workforce. It is often presented as one sentence: "Create a better every day for all people impacted by our business." One can image what a "better every day" can look life for customers—they enjoy their home furnishings, appliances, and accessories. It is distinct from competitors in the furniture business. The one issue we are concerned about is the lack of specification of the end goal. What does the world "look like" when there is a better everyday life created? Given that they have nearly 800 million store visits globally, it could be argued that their vision could have a numeric target. Something like, "We aim to improve the lives of over 1 billion people per year."

Habitat for Humanity

A world where everyone has a decent place to live.[13]

Habitat for Humanity brings people together to build homes, communities, and hope. Homes are built by a volunteer workforce. Habitat makes no profit on the sales.[14] In 2020, 5.9 million people accessed new or improved housing through new home construction, rehabilitation, incremental improvements, and repairs. Since its founding in 1976, the organization has reached the milestone of 35 million people served.[15]

Habitat for Humanity stacks up well on our six criteria. There is an end state to help "everyone in the world." The statement is only 10 words in length, but it sends a powerful message if it is able to achieve its mission. One can visualize the end outcome—a home for everyone. As far as we know, there is no one else in the non-profit world who has such a vision statement. The one significant issue is whether it is achievable; it certainly is challenging to achieve.

Warby Parker

We believe that buying glasses should be easy and fun. It should leave you happy and good looking, with money in your pocket. We believe that everyone has a right to see.[16]

Warby Parker is a US-based retailer of prescription eyeglasses and sunglasses. It is a privately held company with estimates of 2018 sales of $250 million and 1,400 employees.[17] It offers both online and in-store retail locations. A key aspect of the business model was to reduce the price of eyeglasses significantly by breaking the near monopoly power of the existing eyeglass industry structure. The firm notes that "Warby Parker was founded with a rebellious spirit and a lofty objective. To offer designer eyewear at a revolutionary price, while leading the way for socially conscious businesses."[18]

The end state is that everyone has a right to see. They make it possible by offering very low-priced, fashion-forward glasses in an easy and fun environment. While more than one sentence, it uses non-industry common language that makes it easy to comprehend. Also, that the imagery—"easy," "fun"—leaves you happy and looking good is excellent. It is clearly challenging and can inspire the workforce. Arguably one would have specified a very specific target number of individuals rather than say "everyone." Finally, it is distinct: No other eyeglass retailer is positioning their vision in the same way.

Caterpillar

> Our vision is a world in which all people's basic needs – such as shelter, clean water, sanitation, food and reliable power – are fulfilled in an environmentally sustainable way, and a company that improves the quality of the environment and the communities where we live and work.[19]

With 2021 sales and revenues of $51 billion, Caterpillar Inc. is the world's leading manufacturer of construction and mining equipment, diesel and natural gas engines, industrial gas turbines, and diesel-electric locomotives.[20,21] They are ranked 62 on the Fortune 500. They note that their customers use Caterpillar products to build the basic infrastructure that enables higher standards of living so that people have access to water, electricity, roads, bridges, hospitals, schools, and other infrastructure.[22]

We like the Caterpillar vision since it focuses on the end customer and the benefits for the end customer, rather than their true B2B customer who buys their construction and mining equipment. Most B2B firms focus their vision on their immediate customers, but the real societal impact is on the end consumer. While this statement is longer than one sentence, it is highly motivating for the workforce since the aim is to improve the lives of individuals and families by focusing on basic human needs such as shelter, water, and transportation. It is a challenging vision—and may not be fully attainable. Indeed, once again, a specific target may benefit Caterpillar. Also, this statement could use more concrete, visual imagery rather than the abstract concept of fulfilling all people's basic needs.

Smithsonian

> By 2022, the Smithsonian will build on its unique strengths to engage and to inspire more people, where they are, with greater impact, while catalyzing critical conversation on issues affecting our nation and the world.[23]

The Smithsonian Institution is the world's largest museum, education, and research complex. Its massive holdings include over 150 million items. It is comprised of 19 museums, 21 libraries, 9 research centers—all mostly centered in the Washington, DC, area. It has overall 30 million annual visitors (pre-COVID-19) with an annual budget of approximately $1.2 billion.

Its vision statement focuses on "catalyzing critical conversation"—which means that its exhibits and items should lead to conversation about important issues not just in the United States but around the world. It is a lofty goal. It could be argued that this statement cannot be "visualized": What does it mean to have an interesting conversation on an important issue? While it has an energizing quality, it is a rather complex and nuanced set of language. In our view it is both challenging and achievable. However, it could be the case that critical conversations could be started by other museums with similar artifacts. What makes the Smithsonian unique is the breadth and depth of its collection—and we are not sure this is adequately captured in their vision.

Toyota

> Toyota will lead the future mobility society, enriching lives around the world with the safest and most responsible ways of moving people.[24]

Toyota is one of the largest automobile companies in the world. Toyota's group-wide global sales fell 11.3% to 9.528 million vehicles in 2020. That compared with a 15.2% drop at Volkswagen to 9.305 million vehicles. This still makes Toyota the largest automobile company in the world based on unit sales.[25] Sales revenue exceeded $275 billion in 2020. It is frequently on the list of the best places to work and most admired companies. It is one of the first firms to aggressively move into the hybrid, electric vehicle market.

What we find so interesting in the vision statement is the notion that Toyota will lead the future of a mobile society and find the best and most responsible ways to "move people" around. Notice that they do not say automobile company but instead focus on "moving people." Indeed, they do not even say "transportation company," leading to a possible shift in value to software, not hardware, and possible independence from the vehicle itself. It is clearly a future orientation and very challenging. While it is achievable, we believe that more tangible, focused imagery would bring this more abstract statement to life.

Assessing Your Organization's Vision Statement

From the above illustration of six strong vision statements, one can still see room for improvement. Like the mission and purpose statements, the vision statement should be driven from the top of the organization with input from all ranks of employees. It should be "tested" with all key stakeholders, most notably key customers and partners. Below are six questions to use to assess your organization's vision statement.

The six basic questions to ask are as follows:

(1) Does our vision statement have a clear, specific end state or goal?
(2) Is our vision statement one or two sentences in length?
(3) Can our employees and other key stakeholders "visualize" the desired end goal (e.g., a watch on every arm)?
(4) Is the vision statement challenging but attainable?
(5) Does it provide inspiration for key stakeholders, most notably your employees?
(6) Is our vision statement different from our competitors'?

Conclusion

The vision statement goes hand in hand with the mission statement. The mission statement focuses on the "industry" and the "core underlying customer benefit." It answers the basic question of what business we are in. However, it does not specify the end state or the successful completion of the mission. Here is where the vision comes into play. The vision is the desired end goal in the best of all worlds. It rallies the organization and enables the workforce to come to work each day energized by that end target.

Notes

1. "Winning with PepsiCo Positive (pep+)," Pepsico, accessed October 8, 2022, https://www.pepsico.com/about/mission-and-vision.
2. Peter Drucker, *The Essential Drucker* (New York: HarperBusiness, 2008), 61.
3. Confucius and Edward Slingerland, *Essential Analects* (Indianapolis: Hackett Publishing Company, 2006), 14.
4. Bryan Van Norden, *Introduction to Classical Chinese Philosophy* (Indianapolis: Hackett Publishing Company, UK ed.), 42.
5. "SAP Mission, Vision & Values," Comparably, accessed October 8, 2022, https://www.comparably.com/companies/sap/mission.
6. "Frequently Asked Questions," Marriott, accessed October 8, 2022, https://marriott.gcs-web.com/investor-faqs.
7. Andrew M. Carton and Brian J. Lucas, "How can leaders overcome the blurry vision bias? Identifying an antidote to the paradox of vision communication," *Academy of Management Journal* 61, no. 6 (2018): 2106–2129.
8. "The IKEA Vision and Values," IKEA, accessed October 8, 2022, https://www.ikea.com/us/en/this-is-ikea/about-us/vision-and-business-idea-pub7767c393.
9. "IKEA," *Wikipedia*, accessed October 8, 2022, https://en.wikipedia.org/wiki/IKEA.
10. "Gross profit of INGKA Group (IKEA) worldwide from 2009 to 2021," Statista, accessed October 8, 2022, https://www.statista.com/statistics/241801/gross-profit-of-ikea-worldwide/.
11. "Ikea loses 1.5 billion euros to corona crisis," *Retail Detail*, October 6, 2020, https://www.retaildetail.eu/en/news/furniture/ikea-loses-15-billion-euros-corona-crisis.

12. "Vision, Culture, and Values," IKEA, accessed October 8, 2022, https://ikea.jobs.cz/en/vision-culture-and-values/.
13. "About Habitat for Humanity," Habitat for Humanity, accessed October 8, 2022, https://www.habitat.org/about/mission-and-vision.
14. "Frequently Asked Questions," Habitat for Humanity, accessed October 8, 2022, https://www.habitat.org/about/faq.
15. "Habitat serves more than 5.9 million people globally in 2020," Habitat for Humanity, accessed October 8, 2022, https://www.habitat.org/ap/newsroom/2020/habitat-serves-more-59-million-people-globally-2020.
16. "Warby Parker history page," Warby Parker, accessed October 8, 2022, https://www.warbyparker.com/history.
17. "Warby Parker Eyewear," *Inc. Magazine*, accessed October 8, 2022, https://www.inc.com/magazine/201706/tom-foster/warby-parker-eyewear.html.
18. See note 16 above.
19. "Caterpillar Vision Statement," accessed October 8, 2022, https://www.examples.com/vision-statement/caterpillar.html.
20. "About Caterpillar," Caterpillar, accessed October 8, 2022, https://www.caterpillar.com/en/company.html.
21. Ibid.
22. "Strategy & Purpose," Caterpillar, accessed October 8, 2022, https://www.caterpillar.com/en/company/strategy-purpose.html.
23. "Purpose and Vision," Smithsonian, accessed October 8, 2022, https://www.si.edu/about/mission.
24. "Toyota Global Vision," Toyota, accessed October 8, 2022, https://global.toyota/en/company/vision-and-philosophy/global-vision/.
25. "Toyota beats Volkswagen to become world's No.1 car seller in 2020," *CNBC*, January 28, 2021, https://www.cnbc.com/2021/01/28/toyota-beats-volkswagen-to-become-worlds-nopoint1-car-seller-in-2020.html.

Chapter 3

Developing an Organization's Purpose

Introduction

Organizations can have a clear mission and vision but not a clear answer as to the question of *why* the firm exists. Nike may have a clear mission to inspire the athlete in all of us. That is a noble mission. However, it is important to ask, "Why should athletes be inspired?" The answer to this question should be outside the boundaries of the firm and, in particular, linked to a societal benefit. So, why does Nike exist? What is the *specific* societal benefit that Nike delivers? While this question should be posed to Nike executives, we would suggest that improving the mental and physical well-being of athletes is at the core of their purpose. This improvement in health has very tangible societal benefits: Individuals live longer, healthier lives, and society decreases its health care costs. Simply put, healthy and happier citizens improve the functioning of society. While Drucker did not explicitly write on the topic of purpose, he recognized that businesses had a moral and ethical responsibility to improve the functioning of society.[1]

While the mission statement focuses on customer benefits, the purpose state-ment raises the bar to focus on societal benefits. In some organizations, these are very closely related. Amgen's mission, as with many life-science firms, is to improve health and save lives. Here the focus is on the patients who use their medicines. More generally, saving lives not only impacts the patient but also his or her family, community, and the effectiveness of broader healthcare systems. Roche, another life-sciences firm, articulates its purpose as "doing now what patients need next." And, as such, they "believe that good business means a better world."[2]

Twenty years ago, it was rare to find organizations that took the time and effort to define a purpose statement. While there are no formal statistics on purpose statements, our experience suggests that about 25% of Fortune 500 organizations now have a purpose statement or a statement that closely resembles a purpose statement. The reason for this change? While mission statements

Creating the Organization of the Future, 21–30

Emerald Publishing Limited, Howard House, Wagon Lane, Bingley BD16 1WA, UK.

First published as 当德鲁克遇见孔夫子 (*"Setting the Direction for Your Firm"*) by Orient Publishing Center ("OPC"), with Bernard Jaworski and Virginia Cheung, China, 2021. English language translation copyright © 2023, Emerald Publishing Limited. This English language edition published under exclusive licence from OPC by Emerald Publishing Limited. Translated by Bernard Jaworski and Virginia Cheung. The moral right of the copyright holder and translator has been asserted.

All rights of reproduction in any form reserved

doi:10.1108/978-1-83753-216-220231003

articulate that the fundamental customer benefit and vision statements provide the desired end state, neither illustrates how society benefits from the presence of the firm. Yet, it is the societal benefit that is most motivating for employees, customers, and other stakeholders in the community. Not surprisingly, both Drucker and Confucius placed a heavy emphasis on a functioning, harmonious, and effective society.

Peter Drucker noted that crafting a mission statement is hard work, and it is safe to say that the purpose statement is equally hard work.[3] There are three reasons why this is challenging. First, the purpose statement must balance "being realistic" and "a stretch target." If it is too much of a stretch target, it will not be taken seriously by the employees. Second, when employees read the purpose statement, they must be *truly* energized to come to work each day to make it happen. It is not a slogan on the wall. It is one of the fundamental reasons why they joined the organization. Third, some executives may feel that a mission and vision are sufficient to drive the organization into the future. However, nothing could be further from the truth. Confucius recognized the need for positive social change.[4] Today's individuals need more to feel a higher purpose for why their lives matter in the world. Since work is a very large percentage of their daily time, it needs to matter *to them*.

This chapter is organized as follows: We first discuss four characteristics of great purpose statements. Next, we discuss four organizations that have crafted clear and specific purpose statements. We also provide a list of questions for you to consider as you craft your organization's purpose statement.

Motivational Purpose Statements: Getting It Right

Like a mission statement, a purpose statement should be simple, clear, and energizing for the workforce. Here we focus attention on four key characteristics of a great purpose statement: (1) specifies how the organization's activities or products help society (locally or globally) function more efficiently and/or effectively, (2) triggers positive emotions and touches the heart and mind, (3) answers the simple question of why every employee should love to come to work each day, and (4) connects the dots from the firm's products/offers to the societal outcomes.

How Does It Help Society (Globally or Locally) Function Better?

Purpose statements must make it very clear to employees, customers, and other stakeholders how they intend to improve society. This is not a random occurrence; rather, it is baked into the DNA of the company. Siemens, the German conglomerate, with annual revenues of 57 billion euros, started out with a societal focus.[5] Current CEO Joe Kaeser noted that "Siemens was founded on a powerful idea: a company should not only focus on maximizing profit. It should also serve society—with technologies, with its employment practices, with everything it does. This idea is still alive today. Serving society while doing [*sic*] successful and profitable business is at the heart of Siemens' strategy. *It's our company's ultimate purpose.*"[6]

In the case of Siemens, the ability to help society function better as a result of its energy, healthcare, and infrastructure offerings is perhaps very clear-cut. However, other firms need to be very explicit about their role. In the United States, Southwest Airlines defines their purpose as "connecting people to what's important in their lives through friendly, reliable, and low-cost air travel."[7] How does society benefit from this purpose? Southwest focuses on bringing people together for work, vacation, or family gatherings. It is the social fabric that holds society together, and Southwest is doing their part to connect people together.

Importantly, it is possible to be a local provider, and the community of impact is the town or region. So, the purpose does not need to be global (i.e., Siemens) or national (i.e., Southwest), it can be on a regional level in a country or even in a particular city. The key is that it represents the real societal benefit; it is not simply a slogan or public relations campaign.

Touches the Heart and Mind

Roche, the Swiss-based multinational life-sciences firm with revenues of over $60 billion, crafted a six-word purpose statement: "Doing now what patients need next." They elaborate further: "We believe it's urgent to deliver medical solutions right now—even as we develop innovations for the future. We are passionate about transforming patients' lives. We are courageous in both decision and action. And we believe that good business means a better world. That is why we come to work each day. We commit ourselves to scientific rigor, unassailable ethics, and access to medical innovations for all. We do this today to build a better tomorrow. We are proud of who we are, what we do, and how we do it. We are many, working as one across functions, across companies, and across the world."[8]

Energizes the Workforce—Why Employees Love to Come to Work Each Day

Nestle's purpose is to unlock the power of food to enhance the quality of life for everyone, today and for generations to come.[9] As Nestle's US Chief Marketing Officer noted: "As our company changes for the future, our ability to innovate with purpose is how we bring you products you love *and* can feel good about picking up from the grocery store shelves."[10] For their workforce, the broadest aim is to connect food to the quality of life for everyone.

Returning to Siemens, CEO Kaeser told *IndustryWeek* "that the company needed 'an underlying purpose' to unify its variety of businesses. He stressed the role that a higher purpose plays in motivating a workforce, particularly one as vast as Siemens' army of 350,000 employees operating in 203 countries. 'People want to make a difference in life', he said. Making employees part of a quest to serve that purpose, he said, makes them proud to work for a company and is the best way to attract top talent."[11]

Unilever's purpose is to make sustainable living commonplace.[12] They note that "purpose underpins our business. We're embedding it into every part of the company to help us deliver our vision to be the global leader in sustainable business. And our latest figures show it has a significant impact on our performance."[13]

At the core of Unilever reasoning is the belief that brands with purpose grow. They note, "Brands with purpose have three tangible benefits. First, they improve people's health, confidence and well-being. Second, purposeful brands improve the health of the planet. Unilever's aim is to build brands that regenerate nature, fight climate change, and conserve resources for future generations. Finally, purposeful brands contribute to a fairer and more socially inclusive world. Here Unilever believes that their brands that champion human rights stand up for equality and distribute value fairly."[14]

Speaking at the Deutsche Bank conference, CEO Alan Jope said: "We believe the evidence is clear and compelling that brands with purpose grow. In fact, we believe this so strongly that we are prepared to commit that, in the future, every Unilever brand will be a brand with purpose."[15]

He added: "The fantastic work done by brands such as Dove, Vaseline, Seventh Generation, Ben & Jerry's and Brooke Bond shows the huge impact that brands can have in addressing an environmental or social issue. But talking is not enough, it is critical that brands take action and demonstrate their commitment to making a difference."[16]

Connects the Dots to Societal Impact

At Philips, their purpose is to improve people's health and well-being through meaningful innovation. Philips has a specific goal of improving 2.5 billion lives per year by 2030, including 400 million in underserved communities. The Philips solutions are "meaningful innovations" that improve people's health and well-being.[17] Philips' strategy is to be a focused healthcare company—so they could have added "meaningful healthcare innovations" to be more precise. What is interesting about this statement is that they are focused on two communities—society in general and specifically those individuals who, for a variety of reasons, do not have access to world-class healthcare. While the former may be obvious to everyone, the latter is an excellent example of connecting the specific offers to an underserved community.

Motivational Purpose Statements: Examples

In sharp contrast to mission or vision statements which have been used by global firms for nearly 70 years, purpose statements have only gained momentum in the past 20 years. Indeed, only in the past five years have some of the major firms in the world constructed and deployed their purpose statements. These purpose statements have both an internal (e.g., why should I be motivated to work at the end of the day in this organization) and external audience (e.g., why would customers and other stakeholders buy your products?). Below we focus attention on four firms: Chobani, the World Bank, Microsoft, and Johnson & Johnson.

Chobani

Better Food for More People.

Chobani is a US-based food company founded in 2005 by Hamdi Ulukaya who immigrated to the country several years earlier.[18] The initial product was a Greek yogurt and it's now the largest-selling Greek yogurt in the United States. Other products were added over time, and the privately-held company's sales are now estimated to be $1.5 billion.[19,20] As evidence of its employee engagement, 80% of employees at Chobani say it is a great place to work compared to 57% of employees at a typical US-based company.[21] In 2016, the company announced it was giving 10% of the ownership stake to its employees.[22] Due in large part to Ulukaya's life journey, Chobani has a deep commitment to hiring immigrants and refugees. This commitment has come at a cost. After announcing the commitment to refugees, the firm received death threats and boycotts. Approximately 30% of Chobani's 2,000 employees are legally resettled refugees and immigrants.[23]

In an interview with Peter McGuiness, Chobani CMO, he discussed the purpose of Chobani. "'Better Food for More People' started at its founding.[24] And this was based on an insight that people have good taste, they just need good options. Good food is a right, not a privilege." He further noted that Chobani "thought that 'delicious, nutritious, natural, affordable' was the future of food."[25]

This very simple statement passes all four tests of a great purpose statement. It is societal-focused and is not just feeding more people but doing so with better food. The phrase touches the heart since not all people, even in a wealthy country like the United States, are able to consume a sufficient level of basic nutrition each day. The Chobani workforce, as a large immigrant population, often has firsthand experience about the ability to feed their families. Hence, it is a highly motivating goal. And finally, their food is very nutritious—so there is a direct connection between consuming Chobani yogurt and a healthy citizenship.

The World Bank

Bridge Economic Divide Between Rich and Poor Countries.

As noted on its website, the World Bank is an international development organization owned by nearly 200 countries. Its role is to reduce poverty by lending money to the governments of its poorer members to improve their economies and to improve the standard of living of their people. In 1944, the World Bank was established to help rebuild Europe and Japan after World War II. The bank's "projects are essential to helping people become educated, live healthy lives, get jobs, and contribute as active citizens."[26]

The bank's stated purpose is to "bridge the economic divide between poor and rich countries." It does this by turning rich country resources into poor country growth.[27] It has a global purpose to improve the lives of the poorest members of society. For World Bank employees, this purpose provides the motivation to come to work each day. It touches the heart through its stories of how it has helped improve the lives of millions of citizens.[28] Finally, there is a direct connection between its funding of development projects and how the country can better function—and ideally be self-sustaining in the future. The World Bank also serves countries torn apart by conflict and war. They note "fragility, conflict, and violence (FCV) is a critical development challenge that threatens efforts to end extreme poverty, affecting both low- and middle-income countries. By 2030, up to two-thirds of the world's extreme poor will live in FCV settings."[29]

Microsoft

> To empower every person and every organization on the planet to achieve more.[30]

Microsoft needs no formal introduction. While its core strength was desktop software, it has moved aggressively into cloud computing and decreased its emphasis on desktops and hardware. Its shares have grown significantly since Satay Nadella took the helm as CEO in 2014. As of today, Microsoft's annual sales are $140 billion, and its market capitalization is above $1 trillion.

The story of Microsoft's transformation begins with the Nadella appointment. A recent article described the starting point as a "five-month journey that Nadella and the executive team took to re-frame the company's purpose into thirteen succinct words: 'To empower every person and every organization on the planet to achieve more.'"

Microsoft Chief Marketing Officer Chris Capossela noted to the interviewer that the journey to craft purpose had revitalized the company and its employees, leading to a wave of purpose-driven innovation and growth. "Part of the success of the process," the article noted, "was the sense of ownership that the leadership team brought to it, ensuring that it was vetted and tested with the rest of the company to ensure it felt authentic." How did they do that? Capossela explained: "We did a listening tour inside Microsoft, pulling in everyone from new employees, young kids right out of college, to corporate vice presidents, and talking to them in small groups to really understand what words resonated with them and what words didn't. It wasn't just something that the marketing team did off to the side and then just lived off some slides that were posted on a poster somewhere."[31]

The next phase, Capossela continued, involved embedding it into the culture through consistent communication: "We've repeated it at every speech Satya has given, your hear people talk about it all the time in the halls. I don't think that gets done in a week. I think it takes a long time to really own every word, and I'm glad we took the time to make that."[32]

In terms of an assessment, because of Microsoft's enormous reach in the world, the goal of achieving more for individuals and companies is realistic for this particular firm. It could be an enormous stretch for other firms, but, with $140 billion a year in sales, it touches a world population. This idea touches the heart, thus enabling everyone to achieve more and prosper in this world. It is clear that the workforce is energized by this purpose—in part because a large, diverse set of employees help craft the purpose. Finally, arguably, it could use some work on connecting the dots. How exactly do the cloud offerings improve work for individuals and organizations?

Johnson & Johnson

> We blend heart, science, and ingenuity to change the trajectory of health for humanity.

Johnson & Johnson is one of the world's most iconic companies. Founded in 1886, it develops pharmaceuticals, medical devices, and consumer-packaged goods. It is ranked 35 on the Fortune 500 list of largest US companies with revenue of over $80 billion in 2019.[33] It is a highly decentralized collection of over 250 subsidiary companies with products sold in over 175 countries.[34] Widely respected, it is well-known for being a great place to work.[35]

In a recent interview, CEO Alex Gorsky stated that, at Johnson & Johnson, "we have a single purpose: We blend heart, science and ingenuity to change the trajectory of health for humanity." Also, it is not simply a corporate statement, rather it "defines and guides the work we do each and every day." He further notes that "to get there, we're focusing a lot of our attention on helping our employees find and activate their own purpose and connect it with our mission. We've seen that cultivating and developing a deep sense of purpose leads to employees who are more engaged, both personally and professionally. And the data show that focusing on purpose actually leads to many improved outcomes—physically, mentally and emotionally."[36]

Given its life-sciences orientation, it is not surprising that a focus on "changing the trajectory of health for humanity" is squarely centered on improving society. It is interesting to note that they explicitly focus on heart and mind by noting that they "blend heart, science, and ingenuity" to achieve their aim. They connect the dots by noting that it is not simply "science" or "mindset," but these must be translated into meaningful innovations through ingenuity. Ingenuity is defined as clever, original, and inventive.

Finally, it is interesting to note that they have focused individuals on finding their purpose and then aligning it with the overall J &J purpose.

Assessing Your Organization's Purpose Statement

It is very clear that these firms took a good deal of time to develop their purpose statements. The process certainly involved top management—but it also included the input from employees at all levels. In large measure, this is due to the fact that the purpose must resonate with the workforce. They must look at the purpose and "see themselves" as helping to achieve the noble purpose. Keep in mind that Nadella took five months and countless town halls, meetings, and revision. It is very hard work.

To repeat the four basic criteria mentioned earlier, they are as follows:

(1) How does our purpose help society (globally or locally) function better?
(2) Does our purpose touch the hearts and minds of our workforce?
(3) Does our purpose energize our workforce so that they love to come to work each day?
(4) Can we connect the dots of what we do each day with our products, services, and offerings to show how this enables society to function better?

Conclusion

While there is a great deal written on how to develop mission and vision statements, we must also develop a purpose statement to articulate why we exist as an organization. The purpose statement enables the organization to make their human resources as productive and motivated as possible. When properly crafted, this statement is an engine to attract the best talent and have the most significant financial impact. As the Unilever CEO stated, purposeful brands have lasting financial impact.

Notes

1. Peter Drucker, *Management* (New York: Harper & Row, 1973), 319.
2. "Roche Purpose Statement," Roche, accessed October 8, 2022, https://code-of-conduct.roche.com/en/roche-purpose-statement.html.
3. Peter Drucker, *The Practice of Management* (New York: Harper & Row, 1954), 49.
4. Bryn Van Norden, *Introduction to Classical Chinese Philosophy* (Indianapolis: Hackett Publishing Company, UK ed. 2011), 23.
5. "Earnings Release Q4 FY2020," Siemens, November 12, 2020, accessed October 8, 2022, https://assets.new.siemens.com/siemens/assets/api/uuid:6993c2b6-b91e-4285-a8b2-2fefa8199680/HQCOPR202011106056EN.pdf.
6. Siemens Twitter page, accessed October 8, 2022, https://twitter.com/siemens/status/1183004555711266820?lang=en.
7. "About Southwest," Southwest, accessed October 8, 2022, https://www.southwest.com/html/about-southwest/index.html?clk=GFOOTER-ABOUT-ABOUT.
8. See note 2 above.
9. "Our purpose and values," Nestlé, accessed October 8, 2022, https://www.nestle.com/about/how-we-do-business/purpose-values.
10. Alicia Enciso, "Personal, Ever-changing, and Packed with Potential: Why Food Has Purpose," *Medium*, June 3, 2019, https://medium.com/nestle-usa/personal-ever-changing-and-packed-with-potential-why-food-has-purpose-3f8f3c0725d9.

11. Steve Minter, "Siemens CEO Kaeser Puts Energy and Purpose at the Core of Company Changes," *Industry Weekly*, March 1, 2016, https://www.industryweek .com/manufacturing-leader-of-the-week/article/21971189/siemens-ceo-kaeser-puts-energy-and-purpose-at-the-core-of-company-change.
12. "Unilever at a glance," Unilever, accessed October 8, 2022, https://www.unilever. com/our-company/at-a-glance/.
13. "Brands with purpose grow—and here's the proof," Unilever, June 11, 2019, accessed October 8, 2022, https://www.unilever.com/news/news-and-features/ Feature-article/2019/brands-with-purpose-grow-and-here-is-the-proof.html.
14. "How we'll help build a more equitable and inclusive society," Unilever, January 21, 2021, https://www.unilever.com/news/news-and-features/Feature-article/2021/ how-we-will-help-build-a-more-equitable-and-inclusive-society.html.
15. See note 13 above.
16. Ibid.
17. "About Us," Philips, accessed October 8, 2022, https://www.philips.com/a-w/ about.html.
18. "Chobani," *Wikipedia*, accessed October 8, 2022, https://en.wikipedia.org/wiki/ Chobani; "Cultural Revolution," *The Economist*, August 31, 2013.
19. "Chobani unveils largest-ever product line expansion," *Dairy Foods*, November 18, 2019, https://www.dairyfoods.com/articles/93969-chobani-unveils-largest-ever-product-line-expansion.
20. Christopher Doering, "Chobani considering 2021 IPO valuing it at up to $10B, WSJ reports," *Food Dive*, February 5, 2021, https://www.fooddive.com/news/ chobani-considering-2021-ipo-valuing-it-at-up-to-10b-wsj-reports/594609.
21. Great Place to Work 2021 Global Employee Engagement Survey, accessed October 8, 2022, https://www.greatplacetowork.com/certified-company/5003408.
22. Stephanie Strom, "At Chobani, Now It's Not Just the Yogurt That's Rich," *New York Times*, April 26, 2016, https://www.nytimes.com/2016/04/27/business/a-windfall-for-chobani-employees-stakes-in-the-company.html.
23. Christine Lagorio-Chafkin, "This Billion-Dollar Founder Says Hiring Refugees Isn't a Political Act," *Inc. Magazine*, June 2018, https://www.inc.com/magazine/ 201806/christine-lagorio/chobani-yogurt-hamdi-ulukaya-hiring-refugees.html.
24. Afdhel Aziz, "The Power of Purpose: How Peter McGuinness and Chobani Fight for 'Better Food for More People,'" *Forbes*, July 10, 2019, https://www.forbes. com/sites/afdhelaziz/2019/07/10/the-power-of-purpose-how-peter-guinness-and-chobani-are-fighting-for-better-food-for-more-people/?sh=7a88cd536c41.
25. Ibid.
26. "Getting to Know the World Bank," World Bank, accessed October 8, 2022, https:// www.worldbank.org/en/news/feature/2012/07/26/getting_to_know_theworldbank.
27. "The World Bank," *The Balance*, March 4, 2021, https://www.thebalance.com/ the-purpose-of-the-world-bank-3306119.
28. "Results That Change Lives," World Bank, accessed October 8, 2022, https:// www.worldbank.org/en/what-we-do/changinglives.
29. "Conflict and Fragility," International Development Association, accessed October 8, 2022, http://ida.worldbank.org/theme/conflict-and-fragility.
30. "About," Microsoft, accessed March 20, 2023, https://www.microsoft.com/en-us/ about.

31. Afdhel Aziz, "The Power of Purpose: How Microsoft Unlocked Inclusivity to Drive Growth and Innovation," *Forbes*, April 29, 2019, https://www.forbes.com/sites/afdhelaziz/2019/04/29/the-power-of-purpose-how-microsoft-unlocked-inclusivity-to-drive-growth-and-innovation/?sh=39e27f9524e8.

32. Ibid.

33. "Johnson & Johnson on the Fortune 500 rankings," *Fortune*, accessed October 8, 2022, https://fortune.com/company/johnson-johnson/fortune500/.

34. Jacky Chou, "What Companies Does Johnson & Johnson Own?" *Chou Projects*, September 15, 2022. https://chouprojects.com/what-companies-does-johnson-and-johnson-own/.

35. "Johnson & Johnson Named to Glassdoor's 2018 List of Best Places to Work," Johnson & Johnson, December 6, 2017, https://www.jnj.com/latest-news/johnson-johnson-named-glassdoor-best-places-work-2018#:~:text=Johnson%20%26%20Johnson%20has%20been%20named%20among%20the,entirely%20on%20positive%20reviews%20from%20its%20own%20employees.

36. "The Power of Our Credo," Johnson & Johnson, December 13, 2018, https://www.jnj.com/latest-news/johnson-johnson-ceo-alex-gorsky-reflects-on-the-power-of-the-companys-credo.

Chapter 4

Developing an Organization's Values

Introduction

Organizational values are the core principles and beliefs that drive standards of behavior in organizations. When made explicit, they represent the bedrock or foundation for all strategy choices and operations of the firm. They set the boundaries or guardrails for how a company ideally operates to achieve its mission. "Organizations have to have values," Drucker wrote, and building values is an essential component of organizational performance.[1,2] Some values are simply "must have" beliefs that can never be violated (e.g., integrity), while other values are firm-specific and, like culture, uniquely fit the strategy of the firm (e.g., the "fun" value at Workday, or the "fearless" value of Intel, or the "partnership" value of Edward Jones).

Culture focuses on beliefs, practices, rituals, and workflows that shape how work *actually* gets done in the organization. In contrast, values are the guiding light or compass for how work *ideally* gets done. Values should drive every human resource decision—selection, hiring, training, development, career planning, and compensation. Values only work to the extent that employees both "buy into the values" and engage in behavior in ways that reinforce the values. Both Drucker and Confucianism emphasized the importance of actions and behavior that were consistent with values and virtues. At Workday, the "fun value" must be a part of their selection criteria and onboarding process for employees. In sharp contrast, Intel's onboarding process involves "constructive confrontation" training—to provide clear, direct communication—even if it may upset others.[3]

As Peter Drucker noted many years ago, values are to an organization what vitamins are to the human body, as Drucker said, "they are what this organization stands for."[4] They nourish the individuals who work in the organization by providing a Confucian-like set of principles to guide them each day.[5] Even though values are vitally important, some values too often stand for nothing but a desire

Creating the Organization of the Future, 31–42

Emerald Publishing Limited, Howard House, Wagon Lane, Bingley BD16 1WA, UK.

First published as 当德鲁克遇见孔夫子 (*"Setting the Direction for Your Firm"*) by Orient Publishing Center ("OPC"), with Bernard Jaworski and Virginia Cheung, China, 2021. English language translation copyright © 2023, Emerald Publishing Limited. This English language edition published under exclusive licence from OPC by Emerald Publishing Limited. Translated by Bernard Jaworski and Virginia Cheung. The moral right of the copyright holder and translator has been asserted.

All rights of reproduction in any form reserved

doi:10.1108/978-1-83753-216-220231004

to be au courant or, worse still, politically correct.[6] Values such as putting clients first, integrity, or teamwork are often generic statements that provide little guidance for employees. Who would put clients last? Who does not want teamwork? The solution is to put in place a rigorous system to evaluate the behaviors up and down the hierarchy that support these general values. The key point is that stating that one has a teamwork value does little good unless there are widespread, organization-wide actions to support, reinforce, and penalize individuals who engage (or do not engage) in *specific* behaviors that support *their form* of teamwork.

This chapter begins with an articulation of the six criteria to assess organizational values. The challenge for firms is to combine necessary values (e.g., integrity) with values that are truly unique to the firm. The uniqueness is the key since these are the foundation for the strategy choices that follow. Next, we identify six organizations with clear, specific value statements. We then assess each of these organization's value statements against the six criteria. Finally, we provide some guidance on questions that you need to ask yourself as you assess your organization's values.

Clear Organizational Values: Getting It Right

Developing a precise, short list of actionable values is quite hard to do. As noted already, general values, like courage, imagination, and innovation, all sound good on paper, but they need to be understood in the context of *every job* in the organization. Everyone from the frontline employees to the C-suite executives needs a clear understanding of how their behavior supports (or does not support) the values. Below we describe six criteria that can be used to assess an organization's values.

Must Be Meaningful

Values must be connected to the hearts of employees. When properly articulated, they have both a cognitive and an emotional component. Even more common values such as integrity can be brought to life through stories of employees who had to make high-integrity choices that, for a variety of reasons, *at the same time* could have negatively impacted their careers.

Amgen, one of the world's largest biotechnology companies, has a value of competing intensely to win. They describe that value as: "We compete against time, past performance and industry rivals to rapidly achieve high-quality results. Winning requires taking risks. We cannot be lulled into complacency by previous achievements. Though we compete intensely, we maintain high ethical standards and demand integrity in our dealings with competitors, customers, partners, and each other."[7]

Competing intensely to win creates a passionate drive to beat competition. Given the incredible importance of being first to market in the drug industry, employees both understand it (cognition) and are motivated (emotion) to win.

Easy to Understand

For BCG, the world-class management consulting firm, a key value is "expanding the art of the possible." That statement is not easy to understand by itself. However, they describe this value as: "We start with the perspective that the goal is not simply to apply best practice but to invent it. Each client is unique, and there is seldom only one solution. We believe that breakthrough ideas often result from the work of teams seeking to creatively solve real client challenges. We seek to extend the art and science of management by generalizing from our experience."[8] This clear articulation makes the value very clear—it is about new, invented practices rather than simply the reuse of best practices. And how do they create value? By working closely with clients on their most important challenges.

Includes a Combination of Must-Have and Firm-Specific Values

It is rare to find a firm with a completely unique and novel set of values. Often one observes some very basic "table stakes"-type values alongside values that are unique to the firm. Pfizer, the life sciences giant, has several values. Some fall into the table stakes category, like their equity value. Here they describe equity as "we believe that every person deserves to be seen, heard and cared for. This happens when we are inclusive, act with integrity and reduce health care disparities."[9] Most global firms have a value related to diversity, equity, and inclusion. However, Pfizer also has a value of joy, which is quite unusual. Here they describe joy as: "We give ourselves to our work, but it also gives to us. We find joy when we take pride, recognize one another and have fun."[10]

Connected to Specific Behaviors and Expectations of Every Job

The fast fashion company H&M is all about moving quickly to provide "hot" fashion in the marketplace as soon as possible. Thus it is not surprising that they have a value that they refer to as entrepreneurial spirit. They describe this value as, "The day we stop acting like entrepreneurs, we'll be just another fashion company. Our success is built on creativity, innovation and the excitement of making immediate impact. So, whatever our role, we look for opportunity and take initiatives that set our business in motion."[11] This is an excellent link to everyone's job—that everyone needs to innovate in their roles by taking the initiative to move the business forward.

Our observation is that it is often the case that values are not driven down into every role in the organization. Instead, they often provide a general direction, which is a good first step. However, unless every employee can tell you what exactly they do to their behavior in ways that supports the value, the organization is not taking full advantage of their values.

Specific, Not General, Values

Often, firms will develop very general value statements. Indeed, as recently noted in a *Harvard Business Review* article, "55% of all *Fortune* 100 companies claim integrity is a core value, 49% espouse customer satisfaction, and 40% tout teamwork. While these are inarguably good qualities, such terms hardly provide a distinct blueprint for employee behavior. Cookie-cutter values don't set a company apart from competitors; they make it fade into the crowd."[12]

Our view is that general values like integrity, customer satisfaction, and teamwork are all important. However, for these general values to make sense, one needs to be more specific in terms of the nature of these values. For example, take teamwork. There are many different forms of teamwork. For a rowing team, every single stroke is a teamwork activity; however, for a basketball team, there are both individual and team activities. Similarly in one organization, a team may need to be consensus-driven with deep integration yet, in another organization, teamwork could be loosely coupled with decision rights allocated to a single individual.

Uniquely Supports the Strategy of the Firm

One must be able to make a clear connection between the values and the strategy of the firm. For State Farm Insurance, their shared values—quality service and relationships, mutual trust, integrity and financial strength—make perfect sense since their mission is to "help people manage the risks of everyday life, recover from the unexpected, and realize their dreams."[13] As such the strategy of State Farm is built on interpersonal relationships that connect the advisors to the client. Here every single relationship matters as it builds their positioning in the marketplace as the "good neighbor who is always there for you."[14]

Clear Value Statements: Examples

Crafting specific, meaningful, and behavior-driven value statements takes a good deal of time. In the best of worlds, when you read a set of value statements you should be able to identify the firm and the industry. You will notice in the Salesforce values statement that there is a focus on the "industry's most trusted infrastructure," which indicates that it is a technology platform. For Patagonia, they value producing the best clothing products but, at the same time, they want to save the planet, and this leads to sustainable innovation. Since values are so important, they must be driven from the top of the organization. At the same time, the workforce should be involved, consulted, and active in the development of an organization's values. After all, they are the ones who have to live, breathe, and drive the values.

Salesforce

Salesforce is a US-based software-as-a-service vendor in the customer relationship management area. Revenues in 2020 were $17 billion.[15] It a global firm with 68 offices in 21 countries.[16] Its distributed workforce numbers 49,000 employees.[17] The firm is consistently identified as one of the best places to work. It ranked at number two on Fortune's best places to work list in 2021.[18] They believe that a large part of their success is their culture of "Ohana," which is a Hawaiian word for intentional family. Furthermore, this Ohana spirit is guided by four core values that serve as the foundation for their decisions and behaviors.[19] Here is how they describe their four values:

We act as trusted advisors
We earn the trust of our customers, employees, and extended family through transparency, security, compliance, privacy, and performance. And we deliver the industry's most trusted infrastructure.
When our customers succeed, we succeed
So, we champion them to achieve extraordinary things. We innovate and expand our business offerings to provide all our stakeholders with new avenues to achieve ever greater success.
Everyone deserves equal opportunities
We believe everyone should be seen, heard, valued, and empowered to succeed. Hearing diverse perspectives fuels innovation, deepens connections between people, and makes us a better company.
We innovate together
Our customers' input helps us develop products that best serve their business needs. Providing continual technology releases and new initiatives gives our customers a competitive advantage.[20]

Referring to our criteria, one can see that these values are easy to understand and comprehend. Our critique is that while the values signal a few things about the industry (such as their trusted infrastructure), these value statements could relate to any Silicon Valley technology company. Thus, we do not see enough "firm-specific" values in this list. However, we can see that there are specific behaviors that would be associated with each of these values (e.g., customer input drives innovation, everyone should be heard and valued). Lastly, while there are direct links to their strategy (e.g., "providing continual technology releases and new initiatives gives our customers a competitive advantage"), there is room for improvement on these criteria.

Edward Jones

Edward Jones is a financial services firm headquartered in the United States. It has over 15,000 branch offices where financial advisors give advice to individual, long-term investors. It is a privately held partnership with a deep commitment to clients and the communities it serves. It has over $1 trillion under management.[21] Its investment choices are largely conservative (e.g., mutual funds) rather than speculative investments (e.g., day trading of stocks). Its strategy is focused only on individual, not institutional, investors and does so largely through face-to-face meetings. Unlike Fidelity or Charles Schwab, its technology platform is not managed by clients: Rather, all transactions are done through their individual financial advisors.[22]

With this strategy in mind, Edward Jones lives by four core values:

- Our client interests come first.
- We believe in a quality-oriented, long-term investment philosophy.
- We value working in partnership.
- Individuals and their contributions are valued and respected.[23]

These values are meaningful and easy to understand. Clients' interests come first, and valued individual contributions are baseline, table-stakes values. However, the long-term investment strategy and partnership are unique to Edward Jones in the US market. The values—clients' interests first, long-term investments, and partnerships—are all decisions that support the strategy to focus on individual or family investors who are committed to a life-long, very conservative investment strategy. Interestingly, these values gain more meaning when one can identify specific situations where the values were tested and the firm still make a values-led decision. For Edward Jones, that would be a situation in which it put a client's interest first and it was not in Edward Jones' best interest. That is the truest test of the client's first value.

Workday

Workday is an enterprise software platform focused on financial management and human resources. In 2020, revenue for the company was $3.6 billion with year-over-year growth of 28%.[24] The firm is consistently ranked as one of the best places to work. In 2020 Fortune ranked it at number five on its list of the best places to work. Regarding values, they note that "our core values give us a framework for leadership and daily decisions and help us enjoy our time at work. Sounds so simple, but too often companies get caught up in politics, ivory-tower attitudes, and market mania instead of focusing on the things that probably made them successful in the first place."[25] Workday has six core value statements:

Employees
   Most fundamentally, people are the core of our business. Without them, we would not have a business. We hire the best and expect great accomplishments.
Customer Service
   Every investment and decision we make has our customers in mind, and we pull out all stops to make the satisfaction of our customers paramount.
Innovation
   We aim for innovation not only in our development organization but also in the way we approach all aspects of our business.
Integrity
   We say what we mean and mean what we say. We stick to our commitments, treat everyone equitably, and communicate openly and honestly.

Fun
We also feel it's important to have a sense of humor. We like to laugh—it makes our work that much more enjoyable. We also invest in community and company events that help our employees and their families feel a connection to Workday beyond business as usual.

Profitability
Long-term economic success is what helps us provide employees and customers with the best productivity tools, solutions, and services. While important, profitability is not why we exist. Simply put, at Workday we exist to make and provide great products and services.

All of these statements are meaningful and easy to understand. They are written clearly, succinctly, and in plain English. The list includes "must haves" (e.g., profitability, integrity) and firm-specific values (e.g., fun). The specific articulation of the value alone (e.g., innovation) is very general—hence the supporting sentence is necessary to show the exact meaning in a Workday environment (e.g., it is not just about products, but it is about every aspect of the business). One can easily make the connection from the values to specific behaviors for individual jobs. Our view is that the value statements could be improved by more directly tying them to the Workday strategy. While values such as happy employees and satisfied customers are key to the Workday business, that is true of almost any business.

Intel

Intel is one of the iconic firms in Silicon Valley. Founded by Gordon Moore and Robert Noyce in 1968, its core products are semi-conductors.[26] It is the world's largest semiconductor firm with revenues of $79 billion in 2020.[27] With this top-line revenue, Intel is now 45 on the Fortune 500 list.[28] It produces a wide variety of microchips with their most well-known line, the X86 set of processors, that are found in most desktop and notebook computers.[29] It has over 110,000 employees worldwide. Regarding values, they note that "our values guide how we make decisions, treat each other, and serve our customers. They underpin how we achieve our purpose: To create world-changing technology that enriches the lives of every person on earth. More than simply words, our values are the common thread that unites us." In particular, Intel has six core values:

Fearless
We are bold and innovative. We take risks, fail fast, and learn from mistakes to be better, faster, and smarter next time.

Inclusion
We strive to build a culture of belonging. We create a space where everyone can contribute to their fullest potential and deliver their best work. We welcome differences, knowing it makes us better.

Customer-obsessed
   We listen, learn, and anticipate our customers' need to deliver on their ambitions. Our customers' success is our success.
One Intel
   We appreciate, respect, and trust each other. We commit to team over individual success. Innovators at heart, we bring fun to work every day!
Truth and transparency
   We are committed to being open, honest, ethical, and timely with our information and feedback. We constructively challenge in the spirit of getting to the best possible result. We act with uncompromising integrity.
Quality
   We deliver quality and ensure a safe workplace. We have discipline to deliver products and services that our customers and partners can always rely on.[30]

   These values are meaningful, actionable, and easy to understand. They include a blend of must-have (e.g., integrity) and firm-specific values (e.g., fearless, one Intel). It is relatively easy to connect specific behaviors to every job in the organization. Many of these values could apply to other organizations; however, the fearless value is unique and different. It is not a typical organizational value. A second key aspect of their values is "constructive confrontation" to get to the best solutions. This often entails direct and candid conversations, which is not typical for most firms. Finally, while there are some aspects of their values that are tied to their strategy, there is room for improvement on these criteria.

Patagonia

Based in California, Patagonia is well-known as a purpose-driven organization. It is a designer and producer of outdoor clothing for what they term the "silent" sports such as climbing, surfing, skiing, snowboarding, and flyfishing.[31] They state they are in the business of saving the planet.[32] They will use their resources and voice to address the issue of climate change. Hence, they take an activist position. It is a privately held company with estimated revenues of $600 million and around 1,500 employees.[33] With this orientation in mind, Patagonia has four key values:

Build the best product
   Our criteria for the best product rests on function, repairability, and, foremost, durability. Among the most direct ways we can limit ecological impacts is with goods that last for generations or can be recycled so the materials in them remain in use. Making the best product matters for saving the planet.
Cause no unnecessary harm
   We know that our business activity—from lighting stores to dyeing shirts—is part of the problem. We work steadily to change our business practices and share what we've learned. But we recognize that this is not enough. We seek not only to do less harm, but more good.

Use business to protect nature
The challenges we face as a society require leadership. Once we identify a problem, we act. We embrace risk and act to protect and restore the stability, integrity, and beauty of the web of life.
Not bound by convention
Our success—and much of the fun—lies in developing new ways to do things.[34]

These values are meaningful, different from most firms, and easy to understand. While building the best products in a table-stakes value, the other three values are distinctive and support the strategy of the firm. All the values are tied back to their purpose: to save the planet. They are very specific values that avoid the generalities that we observe in other organizations. In our view, this is a best-of-class example of values statements.

Oracle

Oracle is a software company that focuses on database solutions as well as enterprise software. Sales in 2022 were over $42 billion, making it one of the largest technology companies in the world.[35] Currently, it is 91 on the Fortune 500 list of largest firms.[36] It competes with Microsoft, IBM, Amazon Web services, SAP, and several other leading technology firms.[37] It has developed 10 values, which is one of the longer lists of values.

Integrity. We are honest and make responsible decisions. We speak up for what is right.

Customer Satisfaction. Our customers are our top priority. We make every effort to understand their needs.

Mutual Respect. We treat each other with respect and dignity. We value the unique contributions that each individual brings.

Quality. We strive for excellence. We hold ourselves to the highest possible standards and always try to improve.

Teamwork. We work together to make things the best they can be. We collaborate, share ideas, and give constructive feedback.

Fairness. We treat everyone we work with fairly. We do everything we can to make sure our decisions are free from bias.

Communication. We share knowledge effectively with one another. We respect the need for confidentiality regarding certain information.

Compliance. We comply with all laws, regulations, and policies that govern Oracle's business and our own actions.

Innovation. We welcome new ideas and dare to try new things. Problems are solved where creativity and technical expertise meet.

Ethics. We uphold the highest standards of moral behavior and we act ethically at all times.[38]

These values are easy to understand, clear to act on, and cover a wide range of topics. The concern we have with these values is that they could apply to almost any firm. They are largely general in nature and seem to heavily focus on topics like ethics and compliance. It is certainly easy to tie these values to specific on-the-job expectations. However, they are so general it is hard to see how they uniquely support the business strategy of Oracle.

Assessing Your Organization's Values

Similar to previous chapters, we provide a short list of questions that will guide you in the development or the revision of your value statements.

The basic questions to ask are:

(1) Are your value statements meaningful? That is, do they generate both cognitive and emotional reactions for your employees?
(2) Are they easy to understand and comprehend?
(3) Can every employee connect the value statements to their specific activities and role within the organization?
(4) Do you have a combination of must-have and firm-specific values? Which ones are must-have? Which are firm-specific?
(5) Are the value statements specific? If not, do you have a description of the value so that employees can see how this value should work in your organization?
(6) Is there a link between the value statements and your strategy? Which values uniquely drive the strategy of your organization?

Conclusion

Values are perhaps the most abstract of all the setting direction chapters. Remember that values represent the "perfect behaviors" for all employees. But that alone is not the reason to have values. The values must be the bedrock for the strategy of the firm. The values, when properly crafted, clearly link to and support the strategy of the firm.

Notes

1. Peter Drucker, *The Essential Drucker* (New York: HarperBusiness, 2008), 223.
2. See note 1 above. 209.
3. Patrick Lencioni, "Make Your Values Mean Something," *Harvard Business Review*, July 2002, https://hbr.org/2002/07/make-your-values-mean-something.
4. See note 1 above. 210.
5. Analects 2.3; *The Great Learning*; Confucius and Slingerland Edward, *Essential Analects*, (Indianapolis: Hackett Publishing Company, 2006), 4.
6. See note 3 above.
7. "Mission and Values," Amgen, accessed October 8, 2022, https://www.amgen.com/about/mission-and-values.

8. "About BCG," BCG, accessed October 8, 2022, https://www.bcg.com/about/mission/values.
9. "Our Values and Culture," Pfizer, accessed October 8, 2022, https://www.pfizer.com/sites/default/files/investors/financial_reports/annual_reports/2019/our-purpose/our-values-and-culture.
10. Ibid.
11. "Our Values," H&M Group, accessed October 8, 2022, https://hmgroup.com/about-us/our-values/.
12. See note 3 above.
13. "Company Overview," State Farm, https://www.statefarm.com/about-us/company-overview/company-profile/mission.
14. "State Farm Commercials page," State Farm, https://www.statefarm.com/promotions/commercials.
15. "Salesforce Announces Record Fourth Quarter and Full Year Fiscal 2020 Results," Salesforce, accessed October 8, 2022, https://investor.salesforce.com/press-releases/press-release-details/2020/Salesforce-Announces-Record-Fourth-Quarter-and-Full-Year-Fiscal-2020-Results/default.aspx.
16. "Salesforce map of locations," Craft, accessed October 8, 2022, https://craft.co/salesforce/locations.
17. "Salesforce: Number of Employees 2010–2022/CRM," Macrotrends, accessed October 8, 2022, https://www.macrotrends.net/stocks/charts/CRM/salesforce,inc/number-of-employees.
18. "Salesforce is #2 on the FORTUNE 100 Best Companies to Work For List," Salesforce, accessed October 8, 2022, https://www.salesforce.com/news/stories/fortune-salesforce-best-companies-list-2021/.
19. "About Us," Salesforce, accessed October 8, 2022, https://www.salesforce.com/eu/company/about-us/.
20. "Our Story," Salesforce, accessed October 8, 2022, https://www.salesforce.com/company/our-story/.
21. "Edward Jones Review 2022," *Investor Junkie*, accessed October 8, 2022, https://investorjunkie.com/reviews/edward-jones.
22. "Homepage," Edward Jones, accessed October 8, 2022, https://www.edwardjones.com/us-en/homepage.
23. "Top Workplaces," Edward Jones, accessed October 8, 2022, https://topworkplaces.com/company/edward-jones/freep/.
24. "Quarterly results page," Workday, accessed October 8, 2022, https://www.workday.com/en-us/company/about-workday/investor-relations/financial-information.html.
25. "Our Values," Workday, accessed October 8, 2022, https://www.workday.com/en-us/company/about-workday/core-values.html.
26. "Intel," *Wikipedia*, accessed October 8, 2022, https://en.wikipedia.org/wiki/Intel.
27. "Intel Reports Fourth-Quarter and Full-Year 2020 Financial Results," Intel, accessed October 8, 2022, https://www.intel.com/content/www/us/en/newsroom/news/fourth-quarter-full-year-2020-financial-results.
28. John Duff, "Fortune 500: Top 10 Technology Companies You Must Know," *Thomson Data*, accessed October 8, 2022, https://www.thomsondata.com/article/fortune-500-top-10-technology-companies-you-must-know.php.
29. "Intel," *Wikipedia*, accessed October 8, 2022, https://en.wikipedia.org/wiki/Intel.

30. "At Intel, Our Values Define Us," Intel, accessed October 8, 2022, https://www.intel.com/content/www/us/en/corporate-responsibility/our-values.html.
31. "Core Values," Patagonia, accessed October 8, 2022, https://www.patagonia.com.au/pages/our-mission.
32. Ibid.
33. "100 Best Companies to work for," *Fortune*, accessed October 8, 2022, https://fortune.com/best-companies/2019/patagonia/.
34. "Core Values," Patagonia, accessed October 8, 2022, https://www.patagonia.com/core-values/.
35. "Oracle news page," Oracle, accessed October 8, 2022, https://investor.oracle.com/investor-news/news-details/2022/Oracle-Announces-Fiscal-2022-Fourth-Quarter-and-Fiscal-Full-Year-Financial-Results/default.aspx.
36. "Oracle in the Fortune 500 ranking," *Fortune*, accessed October 8, 2022, https://fortune.com/company/oracle/fortune500/.
37. "Peer Insights: Reviews Organized by Markets," Gartner, accessed October 8, 2022, https://www.gartner.com/reviews/market/operational-dbms/vendor/oracle/alternatives.
38. "Policies and Standards," Oracle, accessed October 8, 2022, https://www.oracle.com/corporate/citizenship/values-ethics.html.

Chapter 5

Developing an Organization's Culture

Introduction

What is an organizational culture? An organizational culture is a pattern of shared basic assumptions about how the organization survives and thrives. It has been learned over time and is considered valid and important enough to be taught to new members as the correct way to perceive, think, and feel about what the organization needs to do to be successful. Increasingly firms are making their cultures explicit—written down and documented. This makes the assumption that a public document is meant to be shared, discussed, and modified as environments change.

Why is culture important? Culture impacts all aspects of how employees think and behave within organizations. Drucker had a deep belief that culture of the organization—what he termed "espirit dcorps" was so important that it was everyone's responsibility to nurture and evolve the culture. More specifically, culture impacts such practices as the way the company rewards performance, how it spends money and allocates resources, what resources it cultivates, and how people spend their time at the company. As many CEOs note, culture is the most important aspect of their work environment, and this is where they spend a good deal of their time.[1]

So what is the big deal? Why is a strong culture so hard to develop, manage, and evolve? To begin with, it is often hard to capture the real distinguishing spirit of a culture—what it is that drives people in that culture. Second, it is hard to make cultural statements rich enough and distinctive enough to be meaningful for the organization. Third, it is hard to make culture actionable. These three forces make identifying the organization's current culture—and driving change through a new culture—so very difficult to do. Drucker recognized this challenge by pointing out our natural human tendency is to cling to "yesterday's successes."[2] And Confucius' advocation of communal ritual must be practiced as the

Creating the Organization of the Future, 43–54

Emerald Publishing Limited, Howard House, Wagon Lane, Bingley BD16 1WA, UK.

First published as 当德鲁克遇见孔夫子 ("*Setting the Direction for Your Firm*") by Orient Publishing Center ("OPC"), with Bernard Jaworski and Virginia Cheung, China, 2021. English language translation copyright © 2023, Emerald Publishing Limited. This English language edition published under exclusive licence from OPC by Emerald Publishing Limited. Translated by Bernard Jaworski and Virginia Cheung. The moral right of the copyright holder and translator has been asserted.

All rights of reproduction in any form reserved

doi:10.1108/978-1-83753-216-220231005

responsibility of everyone, fairly and equally, raises even higher requirement for a successful culture transformation.[3]

Similar to previous chapters, we begin with a discussion of the characteristics of great organizational cultures. Here we identify six characteristics of a strong, healthy, and viable culture. Next, we focus on six organizations that have developed strong cultures. Here we identify the specific elements and cultural statements for each firm. These should not simply be "your culture" since each culture needs to fit the unique environment of your firm and industry. Developing and evolving your culture is hard work—and we end the chapter with a discussion of getting started on your journey.

Strong Organizational Cultures: Getting It Right

Developing a strong organizational culture takes a great deal of time and effort. As you think about your corporate culture, consider the following characteristics of great cultures. In particular, we have identified six criteria to assess a culture. A specific organization's culture: (1) is not (and should not) be for everyone, (2) reflects how the company believes it will succeed and why, (3) is connected to specific behaviors and expectations, (4) enables workers to imagine what it would be like to be employed by this organization, (5) identifies points of tension between cultural elements that are recognized and articulated, and (6) takes a position—makes specific bets.

Not for Everyone—A Great Fit for One Segment of the Workforce

When we interviewed the CEO of a small financial services firm, we discovered that he interviewed every single potential new employee and told them, "This will either be the best place you have ever worked—or the worst place you have ever worked." In a sense, that is the outcome of a very strong, powerful, and pervasive culture. It simply impacts everything that is done in the firm. The notion is that some individuals "self-select" and are eager to join, while others flatly reject the position.

As one designs the culture, one needs to think carefully about the exact person one is trying to attract—*and* the person one absolutely does not want to attract. Some organizations focus on "consensus in decision-making"—and every large decision requires everyone to agree. Other organizations focus on majority rule and some, like Netflix, push decision-making responsibilities for very big decisions as low as possible in the organization's hierarchy. Is one decision-making model right? No. It is a question of which fits the desired culture that one wants to nourish.

Reflects How the Company Believes It Will Succeed and Why

Some firms believe that speed and nimbleness are necessary to stay "close to their fast-moving industry." As such, they develop and nurture a culture that is all about speed to market (e.g., the graphics chip industry). Others believe that scale is essential to drive costs down—and they build large organizations that are less nimble (e.g., Boeing, Airbus). In the case of graphics chips, firms want to develop cultures that focus on speed, while the airline industry is much more about learning curves, scale, and new designs with long development cycles. For these firms, operational excellence would be a key element of the culture.

Executive teams need to articulate the specific choices that will make them successful concerning markets, products, services, and go-to-market strategies. Once these are fully articulated, one can then ask, "What type of culture do we need to drive these strategy choices?" In sharp contrast to many authors, we believe that specification of the choices that will give you significant competitive advantage comes first—and the development of culture comes second. Culture supports the strategy.

Connected to Specific Behaviors and Expectations

High-level statements about culture (e.g., curiosity, innovative, team-based, results-oriented, customer driven) are meaningless unless they can be tied to specific behaviors. Take the term "customer-driven" or "customer obsession"—these are often found in the cultural statements of leading global firms. What exactly does this mean? Our earlier research showed that customer-driven firms engage in three specific behaviors: (1) they generate intelligence about the market and their customers, (2) they share this information within the firm—to form an organization-wide view of the market and customers, and (3) they use this information to design products, services, and solutions.[4] Once we know the specific behaviors—generating, sharing and using market/customer intelligence—we can link between a desired cultural characteristic and measurable, trackable behaviors.

One Can Imagine What It Would Be Like to Work in This Organization

When one observes a strong culture in practice, it is quite easy to imagine what it is like to work at that firm. Bain, the well-known global management consulting firm, is one clear example. Bain often scores near the top of the rankings for various "best places to work" assessments.[5] The culture at Bain is supportive and collegial. As one consultant puts it, "We have a phrase that we all live by: A Bainie never lets another Bainie fail. Everyone really does live that motto. If you reach out to another Bainie for support, whether to someone in your office or in another hemisphere, you always get a response that is even more helpful than you would have expected. I'm continuously impressed by the passion my fellow Bainies bring to their jobs and their life outside of work."[6]

Points of Tension Between Cultural Elements Are Recognized and Articulated

Consider a firm that has two clear cultural elements: put customers first and deliver financial results. These are two cultural elements that may create tension.

If one is truly putting customers first, there may be situations where the actions you take are not in the best financial interests of the firm. We have been in situations where some of our best clients have asked us to do consulting work and we felt that we were not their best choice since it was outside of our core strength. If they truly put clients first, we would refer that stream of work to another firm. If they truly put delivering financial results first, we would do the work ourselves.

Takes a Position—Makes Specific Bets

A strong corporate culture makes very specific choices and tradeoffs. Some corporate cultures focus on safety, authority, and order. Other cultures focus on fun, learning, and change. There is no one right culture. Every firm can (and does) have a distinct culture—much like a family unit. However, the key to a strong culture is to let the workforce know the specific intent and principles of your culture. Once known, future talent can then make a clear choice to join an organization with culture A and not an organization with culture B. The key is that the culture must support the firm's strategy in a particular industry context. Nvidia, the high-performing graphics chip firm, is committed to "fostering a culture where talented employees can do their life's work. We provide excellent pay and terrific benefits. Employees enjoy a relaxed setting, with a flexible approach to time off."[7] In sharp contrast, Goldman Sachs is much more focused on survival of the fittest, in an intense, work-centered atmosphere—no one would say that working at Goldman is relaxed.[8] That stated, these cultures work exceptionally well for each firm.

Strong Organizational Cultures: Examples

It is exceptionally difficult to build a great corporate culture. The following six case studies illustrate that it is possible for a wide variety of firms. What is so interesting is that all of the firms "make explicit" their culture. They publish it and discuss it regularly. And the best clearly link behaviors to their cultural statements. They live the culture and evaluate their employees based on how well they embody the culture.

Netflix

Netflix is a US-based content and production company in the entertainment industry. It offers streaming content for audiences (movies, television programs) all over the world except for a few countries.[9] Started as a DVD retail distribution company, the firm reinvented itself many times—from DVDs, to content, to online streaming services, and, ultimately, to a full-blown, Hollywood-style production company competing with the movie studios, Amazon, and other providers of streaming content. In 2021, sales exceeded $29 billion and net income was $5.1 billion. It achieves all this success with a staff of 12,000 employees.[10]

Netflix has one of the most well-known corporate cultures in the United States. In 2009, Reed Hastings, the CEO, published the 125-slide culture deck on the internet.[11] In an interview with Wharton publishing, the Chief Human Resource Officer at the time, Patty McCord, noted: "First of all, Reed and I didn't write it. It was a collaborative document that we did with whoever was in management at the time. It was also a PowerPoint presentation, so it wasn't carved in the lobby, and we didn't publish it in hard copy."[12] A key summary slide of the entire deck is noted in Table 5.1.[13]

Table 5.1 identifies the seven key elements of Netflix culture. Let's return to our six criteria and score Netflix. Clearly, this organization is not a great fit for everyone and does appeal to one segment—those who value self-control, responsibility, and want a sports-team, not a family atmosphere. It clearly reflects how it thinks it will succeed: pushing decisions and responsibility as far down into the

Table 5.1. Netflix Corporate Culture.

1 Values are what we value	We particularly value these nine behaviors and skills: judgment, communication, impact, curiosity, innovation, courage, passion, honesty, selflessness.
2 High performance	Great workplace is stunning colleagues. We're like a prosports team, not a family. We do not measure people by how many hours they work or how much they are in the office.
3 Freedom and responsibility	Our model is to increase employee freedom as we grow, rather than limit it, to continue to attract and nourish innovative people, so we have better chance of sustained success. Flexibility is more important than efficiency in the long term.
4 Context, not control	The best managers figure out how to get great outcomes by setting the appropriate context, rather than by trying to control their people.
5 Highly aligned, loosely coupled	Teamwork effectiveness depends on high performance people and good context. The goal is to be big and fast and flexible.
6 Pay top of market	One outstanding employee gets more done and costs less than two adequate employees. We endeavor to only have outstanding employees.
7 Promotions and development	We develop people by giving them the opportunity to develop themselves, by surrounding them with stunning colleagues and giving them big challenges to work on. Career "planning" not for us.

organization as possible and giving a great deal of autonomy (e.g., it not how many days you work but the results you produce). A key aspect of the culture deck was that Hastings noted that the actual company values are the behaviors and skills that are valued by fellow employees. So, one can observe specific behaviors in the cultural statements of Netflix. It is clear how it would be to work in this company, and it is very choiceful (e.g., people are given freedom, not career planning). Needless to say, Netflix would receive very high scores on all six dimensions.

Cisco

Cisco, a Silicon Valley-based technology company, generated over $51 billion in sales and $11.8 billion in net income in 2022. Their core technology products form the foundation of the internet—including products such as networking hardware and software, telecommunications equipment, and other technology products.[14] It is frequently on "best places to work" lists and has been one of the most prominent Silicon Valley companies over the past 25 years.

Cisco has developed what they term their "conscious culture." CEO Chuck Robbins made all of these initiatives a cornerstone of his tenure since taking over in July 2015. Hence, in Cisco's case—like Netflix—it starts from the top-down. It has three components, the first being *environment*. Here Cisco encourages an atmosphere of dignity, respect, fairness, and equity, with an eye toward diversity and inclusion. The second aspect is Cisco's *characteristics*, or how the company culture is shaped by its behaviors, beliefs, and principles.[15] The third and final component is *experience*—essentially, the direct experiences its employees have with the company, through management, their teams, and the work they do.[16]

Consider the six criteria. The key to seeing that it is not for everyone is centered on the second component, which refers to the characteristics that are specific to Cisco. Cisco believes that its talent is its most important resource—and that the idea of being conscious, aware, and respectful of colleagues is the key to their success. On specific behaviors one could argue that there needs to be more detail in these three statements. Despite our searching of the internet, we could not find a complete list of characteristics that represent the second component. However, one author noted that "one key characteristic that Cisco employees often cite is the company's culture of kindness and giving back—perfectly exemplified by the company's far-reaching CSR efforts."[17] One can imagine what it would be like to work in this organization, although this only becomes apparent by searching the website and reading more articles about Cisco.[18] Furthermore, it is not apparent if there are points of tension between cultural elements that are recognized and articulated. The three components do take a position: make specific bets. The key issue here is that all three components must work together.

Costco

Costco is a US-based "big box" retail store that operates as a chain with membership-only customers. It takes a "warehouse"-style approach—selling bulk consumer goods. It also sells meats, organic foods, and wine.[19] It is ranked #10 on the Fortune 500 list of companies, with revenues of over $226 billion and a net income of $5.8 billion.

For founder Jim Sinegal, that culture of promoting passion, integrity, ownership, and motivation in his employees and ensuring that the customer can trust that they are always getting the best deal by shopping with Costco is the core of the company and the key to its success.[20] "People are happy with a job for more reasons than money," Sinegal has said. "There's generally a pride in the organization. . . .. There's an attitude that there's security, that somebody does care about them, that we're offering careers. We're not offering jobs; we're offering careers."[21] Furthermore, their people-first culture includes encouraging employees to achieve the right work-life balance.[22] The following are the main characteristics of Costco's organizational culture[23]:

(1) Focus on employee satisfaction
(2) Focus on internal collaboration
(3) Focus on employee training and growth
(4) Low pressure related to productivity and performance
(5) A learning environment that provides the best opportunities for learning and growth
(6) Focus on customer service and customer satisfaction

As we review our six criteria, Costco scores high on several of the attributes—but there is still room for improvement. The segment of the workforce that is looking for training, growth, and a supportive atmosphere would do very well at Costco. Keep in mind how different these cultural attributes are compared to Netflix (where everyone is asked to develop their own career path). Clearly, the business model of Costco is customer service, and the Costco culture is focused on keeping both employees and customers very satisfied. We do not know if there is more detail on how these general characteristics are tied to specific behaviors, but that exercise would be very easy to do. They do place bets on specific actions—learning and service ahead of productivity. Interestingly, there are few tensions—all seem to be directed toward the goal of employee development and learning as well as high customer satisfaction. Finally, it is clear what it would be like to work at Costco, a caring, nurturing, and development-oriented culture.

In-N-Out Burger

In-N-Out Burger is a privately-owned, regional burger chain that is largely centered in California and the western section of the United Stated.[24] Since it is privately held there are few details on its financials, but sales are estimated to be approximately $1.07 billion in 2021.[25]

They describe their culture as "ethical values, combined with respect, professionalism, and friendliness, [that] continue to nurture a genuine family-oriented atmosphere. Courtesy and kindness build a team-oriented environment among all our associates, including department members and supervisors. We take pride in all that we due to support our stores and, in turn, our customers, by working together to ensure we provide only the freshest, highest quality foods, and exceptional services at all times."[26] While a fast-food chain, In-N-Out has always paid its employees more than the required minimum wage. Other perks such as paid vacation, flexible scheduling, and a focus on promoting from within keep workers happy. Essentially, they pay very well and give front-line employees the opportunity to be promoted up the corporate ladder.[27]

Again, this is a company that scores well on our criteria. Employees, even if well paid, need to start at the bottom and learn the business from the front-lines—and this career path is not for everyone. The keys to their success are fresh ingredients and a hard-working staff that is all about customer service. It is easy to imagine what it would be to work in one of the restaurants: It is fast-paced, busy, and hard work, but it has the payoff of good wages and career advancement. They clearly state that it is a "genuine, family-oriented atmosphere," which clearly places bets versus the much more sports-oriented environment of Netflix.

PwC

PwC is one of the big 4 accounting firms in the world. With revenue of over $42 billion it is the fifth largest privately held firm in the United States.[28] Its core services are auditing, tax, legal, and advisory services. It is a global firm with offices in over 157 countries. Also, in the context of building a single culture, the challenge is enormous since there are over 284,000 employees worldwide, compared to the 12,000 employees of Netflix.

On the PwC global website, they note that their "values and behaviors define the expectations we have for working together and with clients. Although we come from different backgrounds and cultures across the firm, they are what we all have in common. They capture our shared aspirations and expectations, and guide how we make decisions and treat others. As PwC professionals, we align our actions with the values and behaviors of PwC. We think about the values as a full set—all are equally critical to our success."[29] In particular, PwC has five characteristics that shape their culture.

- We act with integrity. We speak up for what's right, even when that's the harder option.
- We make a difference. We stay informed and proactively look for ways to better our world.
- We care. About each other, about our clients, about empowering everyone to do their best.
- We work together. We know feedback, collaboration and diverse perspectives make our work stronger.
- We reimagine the possible. At PwC, we innovate, we test, we iterate, and we learn along the way.[30]

It is very clear that client success will come from working together, innovating in services, and caring about fellow workers and clients. Not surprisingly this service orientation is critical to their success. In today's world of auditing, integrity is a bedrock foundation that must be maintained—hence, it is not surprising that it is the first characteristic on the list. Making a difference in the world is surprising for us to see since it often shows up in the purpose, not in the culture. That stated, we find it very innovative to be part of the desired PwC culture. All said, it is easy to see what it would look like to be a part of the daily work at PwC.

Hewlett-Packard Enterprise

HP is an iconic firm and brand. It has had challenges over the past 20 decades, but it remains one of the foundational firms in Silicon Valley. In 2015, it split into two businesses. The core HP Inc focuses on printers and related products, while HP Enterprise focuses on servers, storage, and networking products. HP Enterprise has revenues of over $20 billion and has over 59,000 employees.[31]

On the HP Enterprise website, a note says, "Our culture is what defines us as a company: how we act, how we treat others, and how we conduct business. Our employees ignite our culture by continuously demonstrating bias for action, being innovators at heart, and always putting partnerships first."[32] The note continues, "HP aims to create technology that makes life better for everyone, everywhere. By engineering experiences that amaze, HP has a legacy of pushing the boundaries of technology to deliver life-enriching, world-changing innovations at every turn. The company believes that the ultimate driver of its success has been and will always be the power of its people—HP considers its diverse, inclusive global community of employees to be one of its greatest strengths and what truly differentiates it in the marketplace."[33]

It is interesting to note that bias for action and innovation are core components of their culture. Within Silicon Valley it is often "speed" to new innovative products—and staying ahead of competitors—that lead to success. You will also note that its people form a core component of its culture. While these statements sound very reasonable, we are concerned about the originality of these culture statements and specific behaviors that they are expected to drive. Put differently, who does not want "innovations" and "putting partnerships first?" In that respect, these statements are not as "choiceful" as compared to the Netflix ones.

Assessing Your Organization's Culture

Assessing your organization's culture is not an easy task. Remember that a good deal of culture is often unarticulated. So, the first step is to make the culture explicit and documented. Once the organization agrees that they have isolated the six to eight most important culture statements, you can then turn to the key questions. Below are the six questions one needs to ask to evaluate the strength of the organization's culture.

(1) Is the culture a great fit for one segment and a bad fit for other segments of the workforce?
(2) Does the culture reflect how the company believes it will succeed and why?
(3) Have the culture statements tied to specific behaviors and expectations?
(4) Can one imagine what it would be like to work in this organization?
(5) Are critical points of tension between cultural elements recognized and articulated?
(6) Does the culture take a position—making specific bets on certain behaviors—in contrast to other behaviors?

Conclusion

Once the firm sets (or resets) its mission, vision, and purpose, its next task is to evaluate its culture. A key issue is whether the culture as it exists is the "right culture" to support the mission, vision, and purpose. Some cultures are family-oriented and provide very supportive environments (like In-N-Out). Others, like Netflix, focus on the sporting team metaphor in sharp contrast to the family-oriented culture. The fundamental question to ask is, "Is this the right culture to support our strategy as we execute on our mission, vision, and purpose?"

Notes

1. Michael E. Porter and Nitin Nohria, "How CEOs Manage Their Time," *Harvard Business Review*, July–August 2018, https://hbr.org/2018/07/how-ceos-manage-time.
2. Peter Drucker, *Management* (New York: Harper & Row, 1973), 84–85.
3. Poola Tirupati Raju, *Introduction to Comparative Philosophy* (Lincoln: University of Nebraska Press, 1962), 132.
4. Bernard Jaworski and Ajay K. Kohli. "Conducting Field-Based, Discovery-Oriented Research: Lessons from Our Market Orientation Research Experience," *Academy of Marketing Review*, December 2017; Jaworski and Kohli, "Market Orientation: Antecedents and Consequences," *Journal of Marketing* 57 (July 1993), 53–70; Jaworski and Kohli, "Market Orientation: The Construct, Research Propositions, and Managerial Implications," *Journal of Marketing* 54 (April 1990), 1–18; Bernard Jaworski, Ajay K. Kohli, and Ajith Kumar. "MARKOR: A Measure of Market Orientation," *Journal of Marketing Research* 30 (November 1993), 467–478.
5. Jennifer Liu, "These Are the Best Places to Work in 2020, According to Employee Reviews," *CNBC*, December 11, 2019, https://www.cnbc.com/2019/12/11/glassdoor-the-10-best-companies-to-work-for-in-2020.html.
6. Jacquelyn Smith, "Here's What It's REALLY Like to Work at Bain, One of America's Top Employers," *Business Insider*, July 6, 2015, https://www.business insider.com/what-its-like-to-work-at-bain-2015-6.
7. "Life at Nvidia," Nvidia, accessed October 8, 2022, https://www.nvidia.com/en-us/about-nvidia/culture-at-nvidia/.

8. Paul Clarke, "12 Handy Hints for Fitting into Goldman Sachs' Culture," *EFinancial Careers*, March 16, 2016, https://www.efinancialcareers.co.uk/news/2016/03/ten-handy-hints-fitting-goldman-sachs.

9. "Netflix," *Wikipedia*, accessed October 8, 2022, https://en.wikipedia.org/wiki/Netflix.

10. Ibid.

11. "Passion," Netflix, accessed October 8, 2022, https://www.slideshare.net/reed2001/culture-1798664/16-16PassionYou_inspire_others_with_yourthirst.

12. "Learning from Netflix: How to Build a Culture of Freedom and Responsibility," Knowledge at Wharton, May 29, 2018, https://knowledge.wharton.upenn.edu/article/how-netflix-built-its-company-culture/.

13. Reed Hastings, "Culture," SlideShare, August 1, 2009, https://www.slideshare.net/reed2001/culture-1798664.

14. "Cisco Systems," *Wikipedia*, accessed October 8, 2022, https://en.wikipedia.org/wiki/Cisco_Systems.

15. Patrick Moorhead, "How Cisco Fosters A 'Conscious Culture' Within the Company," *Forbes*, May 19, 2019, https://www.forbes.com/sites/patrickmoorhead/2019/03/19/how-cisco-fosters-a-conscious-culture-within-the-company/?sh=66c45bf150b7.

16. Patrick Moorhead, "Why No One Should Be Surprised Cisco Named 'World's Best Workplace' For 2019," *Forbes*, November 1, 2019, https://www.forbes.com/sites/moorinsights/2019/11/01/why-no-one-should-be-surprised-cisco-named-worlds-best-workplace-for-2019/?sh=de97bc338860.

17. See note 14 above.

18. Ibid.

19. "Costco," *Wikipedia*, accessed October 8, 2022, https://en.wikipedia.org/wiki/Costco.

20. Tom Relihan, "How Costco's obsession with culture drove success," MIT Management Sloan School, May 11, 2018, https://mitsloan.mit.edu/ideas-made-to-matter/how-costcos-obsession-culture-drove-success.

21. Ibid.

22. "In a World Dominated by Amazon, Costco is Thriving," *Inc. Magazine*, accessed October 8, 2022, https://www.inc.com/justin-bariso/in-a-world-dominated-by-amazon-costco-is-thriving-they-do-it-by-focusing-on-2-simple-things.html.

23. Abhijeet Pratap, "An Analysis of Costco's Organizational Culture and Human Resource Management," notesmatic, August 25, 2017, https://www.notesmatic.com/an-analysis-of-costcos-organizational-culture-and-human-resource-management/#:~:text=The%20culture%20of%20Costco%20was%20founded%20on%20ethics%2C,been%20played%20by%20Jim%20Sinegal%2C%20co-founder%20of%20Costco.

24. "In-N-Out Burger," *Wikipedia*, accessed October 8, 2022, https://en.wikipedia.org/wiki/In-N-Out_Burger.

25. Ibid.

26. "FAQ page," In-N-Out Burger, accessed October 8, 2022, https://www.in-n-out.com/employment/corporate/faqs.

27. "Why Is In-N-Out Burger So Successful?" *Lemonade Stand*, accessed October 8, 2022, https://blog.lemonadestand.org/why-is-in-n-out-burger-so-successful/.

28. "Pricewaterhouse Coopers," *Wikipedia*, accessed October 8, 2022, https://en.wiki pedia.org/wiki/PricewaterhouseCoopers.

29. "Our Culture," PwC, accessed October 8, 2022, https://www.pwc.com/us/en/careers/why-pwc/our-culture.html.

30. Ibid.

31. "Hewlett-Packard," *Wikipedia*, accessed October 8, 2022, https://en.wikipedia.org/wiki/Hewlett-Packard.

32. "Our Culture," Hewlett Packard Enterprise, accessed October 8, 2022, https://www.hpe.com/us/en/about/diversity/culture.html.

33. "Working at HP," The Muse, accessed October 8, 2022, https://www.themuse.com/profiles/hp.

Chapter 6

Getting Started on the Journey: Mission, Vision, and Purpose

Introduction

We are often asked by executives to either guide them through the mission, vision, and purpose (MVP) process or provide a process that they can use on their own. In this chapter, we describe the process that we have followed when working with client firms. At the same time, we fully recognize that each firm is unique and that the process outlined below may need to be modified to fit the particular industry and organization. Also, keep in mind that we have used the process in nonprofits and the social sector. While these settings provide unique challenges, the general approach has proved effective in these contexts.

When embedding a new process, structure, or MVP, one needs to be keenly aware that there will be a number of individuals who will deeply appreciate the new approach and, often, there will be a sizable minority who will resist the change and/or believe the prior approach did not need replacement. As Peter Drucker noted many years ago, organizations crave stability and resist change. Thus, any process that is followed must begin with making the business case for change. Moreover, as the adoption process unfolds, the C-suite team must communicate the same message an inordinate number of times. Making the business case and using uncommon levels of communication are common to all "leading change" models and simply represent best practices.

In order to bring the process to life, we use three "mini-case studies" to highlight the nuanced differences across organizations. The first is a major unit within a world-class global life science firm based in the United States. The second is for a mid-size technology company based in China. And the third is for a non-profit financial services firm in the United States. For the life science firm, they had an existing MVP, but there was a widely held belief that the market had changed and a new MVP was urgently needed. For the mid-size technology firm

Creating the Organization of the Future, 55–64
Emerald Publishing Limited, Howard House, Wagon Lane, Bingley BD16 1WA, UK.
First published as 当德鲁克遇见孔夫子 ("*Setting the Direction for Your Firm*") by Orient Publishing Center ("OPC"), with Bernard Jaworski and Virginia Cheung, China, 2021. English language translation copyright © 2023, Emerald Publishing Limited. This English language edition published under exclusive licence from OPC by Emerald Publishing Limited. Translated by Bernard Jaworski and Virginia Cheung. The moral right of the copyright holder and translator has been asserted.
All rights of reproduction in any form reserved
doi:10.1108/978-1-83753-216-220231006

there was no MVP in place so the work had to focus first on education, followed closely by workshops. The nonprofit had a mission and vision in place, but the CEO and board recognized the need for a revision. This was largely triggered by increasing pressure from competitors.

The seven-step process has four broad phases. The first phase is focused on making the case for change and the design of the senior leadership team that will develop (or update) the MVP. The second phase is the baseline assessment of current MVP using the criteria identified in each chapter. The third phase is the identification of MVP options, testing options, and selecting the final MVP. The fourth phase is the rollout of the new/revised MVP in the organization.

Below we describe each of the seven steps in more detail and highlight the mini-case study challenges.

Leading Change:
Developing (or Updating) a Mission, Vision, and Purpose

In the final analysis, the membership of the entire organization must be able to understand the new MVP, believe it is necessary, and articulate their individual contribution (and goals) to achieve the MVP. When rolled out and implemented, the new MVP requires an organization-wide transformation. This is not just a "top of the house" exercise. Rather, a firm knows when they have a successful rollout when every employee knows the MVP and is motivated to align their contribution to the MVP. That stated, a key starting point is making sure that everyone knows the rationale for the change. This must be step 1 in the process.

Step 1: Making the Case That Change Is Needed: Why Now?

As Drucker noted, when the theory of the business changes, an organization must reexamine all aspects of its current approach—the mission, vision, purpose, strategy, structure, and any other element of the business. The theory of the business is the key assumptions upon which the business was built. It relates to both the macro-environment and the industry structure in which it competes. However, organizations may be motivated to drive a new MVP due to changes in leadership and/or simple evolution of the business. Below we describe the theory of the business and organizational factors that drive the MVP change as well as forces we have observed that get in the way of change.

Theory of the Business

When a customer's needs and wants change in fundamental ways, it often triggers the need to revisit the MVP. Here we are not focused on gradual changes but on step function changes in the nature of wants. A prime example is the change from traditional mobile phones (e.g., Nokia and Blackberry) to smartphones. New competitors in an industry who possess new technologies to deliver customer value is also a strong catalyst to rethink the MVP. The introduction of Waze largely replaced the traditional paper- or book-based road system maps of a city. Technological innovation by itself can create windows for new players to enter an industry (e.g., booking.com versus travel agencies).

Leadership and Business Evolution

The need for a new MVP can be triggered by leadership changes at the top of the organization. Leaders may be brought in by boards who want a change in direction and/or new markets to be served. These leaders may want to operate with a clean slate—so, rather than simply revisit the strategy, the leaders ask the very basic questions of "what business are we in?" and what does success look like in 5–7 years if we have accomplished our mission?

Interestingly, businesses evolve and over time end up either in a different industry with new segments served or their capabilities to deliver the core customer benefits are new and evolving. IBM has had several major evolutions from hardware, software, and services to a cloud-based business. Netflix is another firm that evolved from DVDs to content and now is a streaming studio. ResMed, the sleep apnea provider, has shifted to a hardware and software firm that monitors patients remotely. They have also invested heavily in software platforms that enables them to reach into assisted living facilities. This new set of capabilities shifted their value creation to be more software-related.

In short, forces related to the macro-environment, the shifting industry structure, leadership change, and business evolution individually or collectively impact the need to modify the MVP to fit the new realities of the business.

Factors That Get in the Way of Change

Many firms—often the ones with modest missions and visions—believe that the mission is more of a check-the-box exercise rather than a true rallying cry for the entire organization. When the CEO and C-suite team do not value the MVP, one should not expect the employees to buy into the MVP. Indeed, an interesting exercise is to ask 10 colleagues to tell you the MVP of the organization. If all 10 know them there is likely to be energy created. If only a handful can recite them, then the MVP probably do not matter in the day-to-day life of employees. Organizational inertia and other seemingly more pressing priorities may lead the management team to let the MVP become outdated in relation to the forces of the marketplace. Another possibility is that the champions of the existing MVP are still a part of the organization and, because of their role in the firm, current leadership does not revisit the MVP.

For the global life science firm, a new unit head was appointed and the function was being built out rapidly. Even though its revenue was over $20 billion per year, this unit was nascent and had the opportunity to "change the rules of the game" for their area of specialization. The new unit head and all of his direct reports were very open to revising their mission and vision. The mid-size technology firm had a CEO who felt the firm was very product-driven and focused its energy on product roadmaps. They did not have a mission, vision, or purpose statement. He felt the time was right for them to establish the MVP. And, finally, the nonprofit was experiencing a great deal of competitive pressure as well as a customer base that was much more digitally enabled. They would never match industry leaders on technology but could outperform them with high-touch customer service. The mission and vision were stale and reflected a theory of the business that no longer existed.

Step 2: Compose Senior Leadership Team

The process must be driven from the top of the organization. We have experienced situations in which it has just been the C-suite team, the C-suite team plus board members, and the head of a major division within the organization. This is not a situation in which a firm sets up a steering team (to guide the effort) and a working team (who does all of the day-to-day work). In our view, the work must be done by the senior leadership team.

For the life science firm, the mission and visioning team was comprised of the C-level executive, his direct reports, and the COO. All regions of the world were covered. In total, the team had about 10 members. All of these team members had been hired in the past 18 months, so there was no legacy commitment to an existing MVP. For the mid-size firm, the CEO organized a series of workshops with the top 15 leaders of the firm. The team was comprised of the entire C-level team and a few key individuals who were one level down in the organizational chart. For the financial services firm, the team was comprised of the board and the C-suite. While the owner of the process was the CEO, the chair of the board played an active, significant role in the process. Approximately 10 people participated in the process of revising their MVP.

Step 3: MVP Baseline Assessment

While step 1 is sufficient to make the case that change needs to occur, it is often good practice to evaluate the current MVP against the criteria noted in earlier chapters. This accomplishes two aims. First, it clearly illustrates how the current mission, vision, and/or purpose statements are insufficient or even problematic. Second, this assessment is part of the rollout of the new/revised MVP noted in step 7 below. It provides a diagnostic rationale for why change was necessary.

Mission Criteria

There are two general approaches that we have employed to assess MVP statements. The first is a general overall assessment. The aim is to get agreement on the rigor and relevance of the existing mission statement. This is followed by a Likert-type scale of the criteria for each concept. This enables the team to pinpoint where improvement is needed. In Fig. 6.1, we show the general assessment for the mission statement. You will notice that we have added behavior anchors as a way to identify specific actions, activities, and behaviors that represent a low, medium, and high score on the mission statement. A high score

Fig. 6.1.   General Assessment of Mission Statement.

on the mission assessment would reflect the behaviors at the high end of the scale. For a score of 8, 9, or 10, we note in Fig. 6.1 that a "firm's mission is clear and precise. It focuses attention heavily on its customers and the impact of the organization on society. It energizes employees on a common goal. Employees consistently behave in ways that are supportive of mission."

This general assessment is then followed by six key questions that aim to provide more specific diagnostic information on specific areas to improve. The six general criteria can be assessed on standard strongly agree (5 points) and strongly disagree scale items (1 point).

(1) Our mission statement focuses on the core customer benefit that we deliver and not on any existing product or technology.
(2) Our mission statement specifies our target customer.
(3) Our mission statement is short—one to two sentences.
(4) Our mission statement fits the theory of the business.
(5) Our mission statement inspires our workforce.
(6) Every worker can see how their roles can support the mission.

Focusing on products or technology means that we are limiting ourselves to the current historical period. In sharp contrast, a customer benefit-focused mission statement can last years or decades. Product- and technology-focused statements almost by definition have a limited shelf life. A one-sentence mission statement is, all else being equal, memorable: easy to repeat and recall. Hence, it facilitates any alignment exercise so that everyone can see how they support the mission. The essential point is that the mission is the first task of management, and its core purpose is to answer the question "what business are we in?" from a customer (not internal) perspective.

Vision Criteria

Similar to the mission statement, the vision assessment has two parts. The first part is the general assessment (reflected in Fig. 6.2) and the second is the itemized assessment based on criteria noted in Chapter 2. Regarding the general assessment, we can see in Fig. 6.2 that the vision assessment includes a very clear target goal and that the goal is challenging but attainable. We should note that it is not easy to specify a clear end state; however, without this clear future state, we do not know how to chart our progress.

Regarding the specific criteria assessment, we noted that vision statements can be evaluated in terms of six dimensions. Again, a strongly-agree and strongly-disagree scale can be used to make this assessment. The six diagnostic questions are the following:

(1) Our vision statement specifies a clear end state.
(2) Our vision statement is concise—ideally one sentence.
(3) Our vision evokes a picture of the future through image-based language.
(4) Our vision inspires our workforce.
(5) Our vision is very challenging, yet achievable.
(6) Our vision is distinct from our major competitors.

A clear end state is easier when the target of your efforts is clearly measurable (e.g., the number of people who live in poverty, the number of individuals who are treated by your medical device, or the carbon footprint of energy producers). However, for some areas, the measurement of societal impact may be hard to quantify (e.g., beauty products). Yet without a clear aspiration or goal one can reach different conclusions about societal impact.

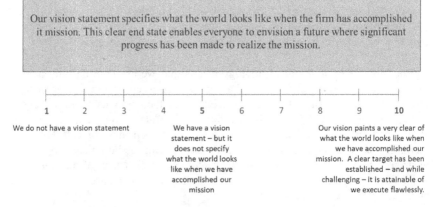

Fig. 6.2.   General Assessment of Vision Statement.

Purpose Criteria

Taking a look at Fig. 6.3, a well-structured purpose statement articulates how the organization improves society. It answers the key question "why do we exist?" or "would any care if we disappeared or failed to operate?" When this is done well—it isn't simply a reason for being—a well-structured purpose statement attracts and retains talent. Increasingly, individuals want to be part of purpose-driven organizations that make the world a better place.

Similarly, regarding the more itemized criteria, there are four key evaluation statements. They are the following:

(1) Our purpose specifies how the organization's activities or products help society (locally or globally) function more efficiently and/or effectively.
(2) Our purpose triggers positive emotions and touches the heart and mind.
(3) Our purpose answers the simple question of why every employee should love to come to work each day.
(4) Our purpose connects the dots from the firm's products/offers to the societal outcomes.

For the large life science firm, the exercise involved evaluating the previous mission and vision statements against six characteristics of great mission and vision statements. This was followed by a lively discussion in which statements did not meet the criteria and suggestions were made for improvement. Step 3 blended a bit with step 4 since participants started to suggest potential MVP statements. For the mid-size technology firm, the statements did not exist so step 3 was skipped. However, these general and specific criteria were widely discussed during step 4. For the small financial services firm, their existing MVP statements were quite general and lacked specificity so very quickly the team moved into step 4.

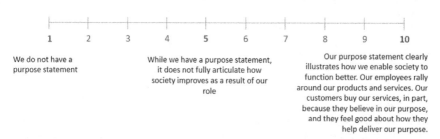

Fig. 6.3.   General Assessment of Purpose Statement.

Step 4: Crafting a Few Legitimate Options

Our experience is that while the synchronization of mission, vision, and purpose statements must be the goal, the process at step 4 should be sequential. We found it is simply too difficult to try to perfectly craft each statement and evaluate how the three fit together. Our recommendation is to begin with the mission followed by vision and purpose. After completing three to four solid drafts of each of the three statements, one can then evaluate how well they fit together. By implication, one cannot complete a mission statement exercise and say it is "final." Instead, once you complete the vision and purpose statements you can then return to the mission statement to evaluate the "degree of fit" of each statement with one another. In all of our experiences, this "working back and forth" between mission, vision, and purpose statements is the way that the process works best.

For the life science firm, the process began by prioritizing the industry, target, core benefit, and dominant therapeutic approach to deliver the benefit. Here the team drafted three alternative mission statements reflecting these choices. Next the team drafted three distinct vision statements. Stepping back from this work, the team could see which mission statements "matched" a particular vision statement. The key is that they needed to work in tandem to tell a story. Certain mission statements only fit with certain vision statements. The same approximate process was followed by the high-tech company and the financial services firm. For the high-tech firm, we crafted several versions of the MVP. Fairly quickly we settled on one of the options and then drafted several versions of that option (we describe this process in step 6 below). The key for the financial services firm was to articulate a mission that truly reflected their very distinctive approach and the community they served. The community they served—that is, the segment focused upon—was very unique and needed to be highlighted in the mission and vision statements.

Step 5: Test MVP Options With a Variety of Key Stakeholders

Interestingly, we have found that the vast majority of our work with C-level teams did *not* involve "testing" the mission, vision, and purpose statements with a subset of employees, customers, investors, or other stakeholders. We have been thinking about this issue and have reached the conclusion that, on balance, this is a C-level team responsibility. Indeed, one can even imagine situations in which the C-level team town hall "tests" of a couple of mission options would leave some employees with the sense that the senior team does not know where to take the company. Indeed, in a worst-case scenario, they could lose confidence in the team. The reaction of town hall participants could be: "Isn't this the responsibility of the senior team to set the mission, vision, and strategy?" Hence, for many situations, testing options is not recommended.

However, if the C-level team does decide to get feedback and "test" options with key stakeholders (such as customers, employees, or relevant stakeholders), there are a few key tips to keep in mind. First, feedback should not be general (e.g., what is your view of this mission statement?). Instead, the relevant stakeholder group should be informed of the criteria. Then they should be asked to rate the mission on the (1) the general assessment above and (2) the specific criteria. Second, test the statements with the direct reports of the C-suite. This is consistent with the Drucker view that it is often the next generation of leaders—the next in line to succession—who have to adopt and execute MVP. So, they must be on board. Third, the team may wish to test this with the board. Given the significance of the mission, vision, and purpose in driving strategy and execution, this clearly can be a board-level conversation and refinement.

To conclude, in our opinion, this testing step is optional and must be done on a case-by-case basis. Based on client work to date, if given clear criteria, the senior team has consistently done an excellent job of crafting these three statements. The key is the refinement, integration, and internal debates per step 6 below.

Step 6: Select, Refine, and Ratify Chosen MVP

Once the MVP are chosen, there is often a phase that involves "refining" each of the statements. Here specific word choices matter. Some may downplay this activity as "wordsmithing," but it is much more than that. Indeed, this conversation is often energizing for the team since they want to select the best word possible.

For the life science firm, over a series of workshops the team mobilized on key mission and vision statements. Here the team carefully tweaked language to finalize statements that best reflect the messages they wanted to communicate. In the case of the high-tech firm, the CEO and our team refined the statements over a series of exchanges. The CEO finally made the call on the final version. In the case of the financial services firm, we reached consensus during the workshops and ratified everything as a group.

Step 7: Rollout and Institutionalization

All of this work does little good unless the entire organization buys into the MVP and is willing to support them through their job activities. The aim is to align the entire workforce with the MVP.

The first step in the process is to build a communication rollout plan. This plan includes: (1) details on the process that was followed by the C-level team, (2) the team composition (why this group?), (3) why were these particular MVP chosen?, (4) often details on the specific words and what they mean is important to share, and (5) the plan moving forward to embed the MVP across the entire organization.

In the case of the life science firm, once the C-suite team agreed on the mission, vision, and purpose, the next step was to conduct a half-day workshop with the organization (N = 60 but plans to scale to several hundred) to communicate the MVP and align each individual role with the MVP. Importantly, all regions of the world participated during this online workshop.

During the workshop, the C-suite team articulated the process that was followed, identified team membership, and described the iterative nature of the work and the selection of the final statements. Great care was taken to explain the specific word choices—and which alternatives were eliminated—to illustrate both the dialogue and care that led to the final choices. After this detailed account, the participants were able to comment through a word-cloud exercise their reactions to the statements. The responses were overwhelmingly positive. A few questions did emerge, and these were handled by the team. Again, one is never going to get 100% buy in; however, one is certainly aiming for a large majority to buy into the work.

Next, the workshop focused on a contribution exercise. This is based on Drucker's view that job descriptions often place constraints on individuals and do not take into account the individual's strength and full potential. The notion is that, once the individual worker understands and internalizes the MVP, he or she can align his or her role and individual objectives to the MVP. The core belief is that self-control is the most powerful form of control: So, you want the individuals to begin the alignment discussion by identifying goals to support the MVP. The key question is, "What can I do to support the Mission and Vision? How can I support my business unit, my team, my boss....?" This goes beyond the job description and focuses on identifying individual strengths and resulting behaviors that can support my environment. This is not a one-time activity; rather, it needs to be repeated on a regular basis.

Conclusion

Drucker noted that every three years an executive team should go off-site and ask themselves the basic question, "If we were going to start the business over gain, knowing what we know now, what would we do?" This analysis may lead the team to abandon core products, work processes, pricing approaches, or distribution approaches. However, this question can also lead one to re-examine the core strategy or even the MVP. We began this chapter by noting that if the theory of the business changes—that is, the core assumptions on which the business is built—then it is completely appropriate to re-examine the mission, vision, and purpose.

In this chapter, we provided an overview of a seven-step process that works. We have conducted these workshops in a variety of firms and have highlighted three mini-case studies. One overall message that we want to make very clear is transparency. If the entire workforce is able to see the process that was followed (its rigor and thoughtfulness), this will go a long way to reassure the workforce that the organization is headed in the right direction. That stated, these seven steps are guidelines, and you may find it useful to customize this process to fit your individual firm's needs.

Chapter 7

Getting Started on the Journey: Culture and Values

Introduction

The previous chapter focused on getting started on the journey to develop (or revise) one's mission, vision, and purpose. We noted that the trigger for this reexamination is most often the result of changes in the theory of the business—the industry structure or macro-environment forces—that impact the evolution of the business. We have observed cultural and values reassessment going hand-in-hand with a reconsideration of the MVP. That was the case with the mid-size Chinese firm. However, we have also been involved in work to revisit the culture and/or values when the firm's MVP has remained the same. In one case, the nonprofit firm had not established a set of values, so the exercise only focused on values.

Values and culture often work hand in hand. In some situations, the values are the visible "code of beliefs and standards" that create the foundation for any activity of the firm: from setting the strategy to specific commercial tactics. Similarly, the culture of the company—which is sometimes stated and sometimes implicit—involves the artifacts, norms, and ways of operating that also set the foundation for activities. The key difference is that these values are always positive and aspirational—and provide the principles and guideposts for how one should behave in the organization. Whereas the culture could be very positive or very negative, the culture "exists" within an organization and shapes the behavior of every employee.

In the best situation, values and culture are aligned to shape behaviors that will help drive organizational success. However, there are clear situations in which the culture of the organization is completely inconsistent with the espoused values. Take the example of Wells Fargo, which agreed to pay $3 billion to resolve investigations into sales practice involving opening millions of accounts without

Creating the Organization of the Future, 65–74

Emerald Publishing Limited, Howard House, Wagon Lane, Bingley BD16 1WA, UK.

First published as 当德鲁克遇见孔夫子 (*"Setting the Direction for Your Firm"*) by Orient Publishing Center ("OPC"), with Bernard Jaworski and Virginia Cheung, China, 2021. English language translation copyright © 2023, Emerald Publishing Limited. This English language edition published under exclusive licence from OPC by Emerald Publishing Limited. Translated by Bernard Jaworski and Virginia Cheung. The moral right of the copyright holder and translator has been asserted.

All rights of reproduction in any form reserved

doi:10.1108/978-1-83753-216-220231007

customer authorization. Yet their corporate values at the time stressed customer centricity. Indeed, in an article in *Forbes*, the bank noted one of its values statements: "We believe shareholders come last. If we do what's right for our team members, customers, and communities, then—and only then—will our shareholders see us as a great investment."[1]

In this chapter, we introduce an eight-step process to create (or revise) an organizations' value and culture. This is similar to the process followed for the MVP journey, yet it is distinctive because it does employ a steering and working team model that are familiar to most leading change frameworks. The process begins with a case for change. This is followed by the formation of a steering team and a working team. Since the working team is critical to the success of this intervention, we spend more time reflecting on team design, launch, and process. Also, in crafting the values and culture, it is often the case that a "longer list" is established and then reduced to the final set. This is in contrast to the "option choice" decision in the MVP journey. We conclude with the selection of the final version of the values and cultural statement along with suggestions on the rollout.

The Journey: An Eight-Step Process to Identify (or Refine) Your Culture and Values

It has been our experience that the process of identifying the best set of values for the organization is easier than the specification of the culture. The reason why this is easier largely rests with the hidden aspects of culture that need to be identified. In the case of the life science firm, they were just getting started on the journey, so culture had not been established. But for the nonprofit—a social cause organization that had been running for several years—the culture did exist, but the process to surface it took time, effort, and skill. We will illustrate some of the differences between values and culture as we consider the eight-step process.

Similar to MVP, a case needs to be made for change. It could be externally driven: significant changes in customer tastes, new competitors, or the transformative role of digital technologies in the industry. In some cases, the firm has responded by revising its MVP, which, in turn, triggers the conversation about how well the values and culture support the MVP. Steps 2 and 3 focus on building and launching the steering and working teams. Steps 4 and 5 are the discovery and crafting phases in which the output is a "preliminary list" of value statements and culture elements. In the case of one nonprofit, the list of values was 12, which were eventually narrowed to seven. In the final three steps, the values and cultural elements are refined, finalized, and rolled out to the entire organization.

Step 1: Make the Case for Change

Making the case for an organization's values or an articulation of the culture is a different situation than one in which an organization decides to revise its values or culture. In the case of the former, it is often the natural progression of an organization. As Drucker noted, all organizations need values to guide the behavior of employees. For many new firms, the management team recognizes the importance of values but has simply not articulated a values statement. However, the revision is a different story since the values revision is infrequent and changing culture is notoriously difficult. Here the organization members need to "buy in" to the updating process.

As noted above, there are typically two triggers for the revision of values and culture. The first is an external shock to the system: a massive regulatory change, new competitors with a different technology platform, or a fundamental shift in buyer behavior. The second trigger is the revision of the mission, vision, or purpose. Here the notion is that the culture and values need to support the MVP. So, the key question is whether the current culture and values are limiting the attainment of the new MVP.

Step 2: Form a Strong Steering Team

A steering team's role is to provide oversight, guidance, and direction for the team that will revise the culture and values. The steering team also typically has the right to make the call on the final set of values and culture statements. The rationale for both a steering team and working team is that, in contrast to MVP, the culture values are "how we work and what we value" as compared to the selection of the right direction-setting characteristics of an MVP. The later decisions sit comfortably in the office of the CEO. Yet, "how we work and what we value" can be more of a collective viewpoint reflecting the broad workforce. Thus, gaining organization-wide input is a critical stage of the process. Again, the steering team will have decision rights to confirm the final set of values and cultural elements.

Three criteria should be taken into consideration as you form your steering team. First, the process needs to be driven by C-level executives. This is another top-of-the- house set of decisions that will shape the future of the organization. Here it is best to have two to three members of the C-team on the steering team. This provides the right amount of senior engagement and signals that it is a cross-functional, company-wide effort. Second, the team should be small in number (often three to four individuals). Again, assuming the individuals are C-level, there is no need to have a 10-member team. A small powerful coalition is sufficient. Third, the chief people or talent officer should be part of the coalition. The values and culture of an organization also are intimately tied to various competency models (e.g., a competency such as teamwork or putting customers first). So, the involvement of the chief talent officer increases the probability there will be downstream alignment with desired leadership behaviors.

Step 3: Select, Design, and Launch the Working Team

The working team is responsible for conducting the current baseline assessment of the culture and values, drafting a new (or revised) preliminary list of culture elements and values, narrowing the list through some form of stakeholder feedback, and providing a final set of recommendations to the steering team. Given that this process typically takes weeks if not months, it is a good decision to follow best practices in new team formation. In particular, the working team needs to work through three team phases: (1) the design of the working team, (2) the launch of the team, and (3) team process.

Regarding team design, the steering team needs to address five key questions on team composition. First, what is the compelling purpose for the team? Why this team now? Second, the steering team needs to identify the right team membership. Many factors shape this choice including factors related to skill set, motivation, and time commitment of the members. At the same time, one also needs to think about representation from co-workers' perspectives: Are these team members some of our best talent? Do they represent the broad organization? Are they respected within the organization? Third, what is the right structure and role design? Who is the working team's chairperson? What roles need to be assigned a research role? What is the specific timeline for the effort? Not only the start and finish dates but also key dates on steering team check-ins, workshops to get feedback on work in progress, and tie-in to rollout plans. What type of support will the steering team provide (resources, support personnel, and acknowledgment of working team efforts)?

As we all know, launching a new team should be based on some best practice recommendations. First, one needs to articulate the overall goals of the project and the exact form of the deliverables. Is this going to be a written document, a PowerPoint deck, and/or a video summary of the work? Second, one needs to articulate the specific tasks to be performed and the role of each individual team member. Here each individual member should be prepared to discuss strengths, preferred working style, and the specific tasks that best utilize their abilities. Here the committee chairperson should reflect on the overall skills, strengths, and jobs to be done, and make sure that each individual knows his or her role (e.g., researching competitor value statements, conducting the workshops to narrow the preliminary list to a short list, etc.).

The team also has to have a conversation about the ways they will work together. This involves five specific considerations. First, what is the cadence of their communication: How often? What format? Second, how will the team make decisions on key issues (e.g., how to narrow from a preliminary list to a final list? Is it majority rule or some other process?)? Third, how will the team share information? How often will the team meet? What sharing platforms such as Dropbox are they using? How does the team maintain version control of the key documents? Fourth, conflict or disagreements are inevitable: How will the team deal with conflict resolution? Finally, what is our best working style? How does each of us like to work?

For the nonprofit team, the working team was comprised of four team members. They reflected the diversity of roles—from central headquarters to the regional offices. All four members held different job titles and were located across the United States. The team established the working cadence of the group, the desired work product, and roles on the project.

Step 4: Culture and Values Baseline Assessment

Assuming that your organization has existing values and culture statements, the first task of the working team is to pull together a baseline assessment of where you are now. Similar to the MVP, the assessment operates at the (a) general level and (b) at the level of the specific criteria.

Values Assessment

Taking a look at Fig. 7.1, we observe a generalized measure of values. The core notion is that organizations with a strong values orientation truly live and breathe the values. Our general statement captures the idea that employees in the organization live by a core set of values, animated by the belief that an organization needs values "as a human body needs vitamins and minerals." A high score on being values-led would mean that values are the North Star that guides the firm. In this organization there are regular discussions related to adhering to its values. All employees "buy into" and "live" the values. Those that do not are removed from the organization, even if they are high performers. Indeed, this is almost the litmus test of a values-led company; when the organization has high performers who are not living the values, they are reprimanded, demoted, assigned improvement plans, or asked to leave.

Regarding the scale items below, there are three key characteristics that one looks for in every single values statement. First, employees comprehend, understand, and live the values. Second, the values are perceived as meaningful insofar as they connect emotionally with each employee. Third, they understand when their behavior is consistent or inconsistent with the values. Thus, each value statement can be evaluated on cognitive, emotional, and behavioral grounds.

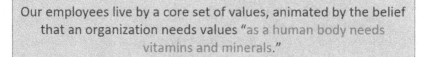

Our employees live by a core set of values, animated by the belief that an organization needs values "as a human body needs vitamins and minerals."

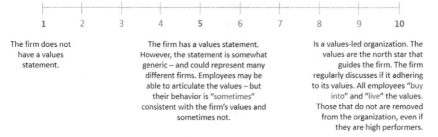

1	2	3	4	5	6	7	8	9	10
The firm does not have a values statement.			The firm has a values statement. However, the statement is somewhat generic – and could represent many different firms. Employees may be able to articulate the values – but their behavior is "sometimes" consistent with the firm's values and sometimes not.				Is a values-led organization. The values are the north star that guides the firm. The firm regularly discusses if it adhering to its values. All employees "buy into" and "live" the values. Those that do not are removed from the organization, even if they are high performers.		

Fig. 7.1.   Assessing Organizational Values.

Finally, the values support the activities of the organization–the strategy, operations, and execution.

(1) Our values speak to what is meaningful to our employees.
(2) Our values are easy to understand and comprehend.
(3) Our values are comprised of a mixture of must-have values applicable to many firms and some values that are truly unique to our firm.
(4) Our values can easily be translated into behaviors that resonate with every role within our firm.
(5) Our values are very specific; they are not values in general.
(6) Our values clearly are linked to and support our firm-wide strategy.

Culture Assessment
Finally, like the values assessment, the cultural assessment can also be in summary form (Fig. 7.2) or one can decompose the specific criteria to evaluate each cultural element. In Fig. 7.2, we begin with the general statement that "our culture is based on a strong set of values, beliefs, norms, and rituals that shape the behavior of employees. We have a strong culture in the sense that almost everyone knows how things work in this organization. Our culture is a great fit for some people and a terrible fit for others." At the high end of the general assessment scale, we observe organizations that have a strong, positive organizational culture that supports the strategy. The culture enables new employees to imagine what it would be like to be employed by the organization. We have observed that our culture is a perfect fit for some people and a terrible fit for others. Throughout our organization there is a widespread belief that our culture is one of the secrets of our success.

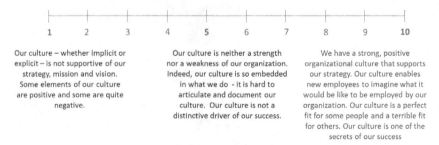

Fig. 7.2.   Assessing Organizational Culture.

Turning to the specific question for each cultural element, we can see that placing specific bets on well-crafted, specific cultural elements enables workers to make a choice on the degree of fit of their work habits and patterns with that of the firm. Similarly, the firm is also trying to assess cultural fit. Importantly, the culture is key to the firm's success: It reflects "what we believe we need to do" to be successful. Like values, the working team should be able to tie the specific behaviors of all employees to the culture elements. Specifically, the six criteria are as follows:

(1) Our culture is not (and should not be) for everyone.
(2) Our culture reflects what we believe we need to do to be successful.
(3) Our culture is connected to specific behaviors and expectations.
(4) Our culture enables workers to imagine what it would be like to be employed by our organization.
(5) Our culture acknowledges, recognizes, and articulates some potential points of tension between cultural elements.
(6) Our culture clearly takes a position on what behaviors we are driving–thus we make explicit bets.

For the nonprofit firm, there were no values at the start. So, to start the process the top 30 leaders were given a basic workshop on values and culture. Key definitions where shared and the concepts were discussed. Sample value and cultural statements that scored well on the criteria were identified and discussed. As a result, this "top of the house" set of leaders could "see" what good looked like. Also stressed during this workshop was the idea that the values must support the mission, vision, and purpose of the organization. Since a leadership competency model has just been rolled out, we also needed to discuss how the leadership competency model supported the values and how the values, in turn, should support the leadership competency model. This conversation was quite lively since topics such as putting customers first or communication appeared in both the values and leadership competencies.

After a good deal of discussion, each participant was asked to identify four values from a list of over 40. Each person also had the option of adding to the list. The result was a list of 12 values that all received at least five votes. This was the starting point of their "crafting approach" in step 5.

In general, however, if values and cultural statements do exist, the working team needs to establish an approach to evaluate "where we are now" (both general assessment and specific criteria). There are a number of options to consider and it really depends on the needs of the organization. If downstream "buy-in" is going to be a challenge, then one needs to spend more time getting the organization involved at this stage. If they can give input early—their assessments, discussions, and feedback with working team—it will go a long way to getting commitment during the rollout stage.

Key issues for the working team at this point are (1) which specific employees and groups do we involve in the assessment? (2) setting expectations from employees who were queried (e.g., steering team has decision rights, we are seeking input from you) and (3) how the results will be analyzed and summarized.

Step 5: Crafting a Preliminary Version of Culture and Values

At the end of step 4, the working team will have a working list of values statements and cultural elements. This preliminary list is either as a result of the workshop approach noted above or as a result of a broader assessment of employees evaluation/assessment of the current values and culture statements. Rather than attempt to shorten this list at this stage, the next step is the definition of the value or cultural element. Here it may need to be defined for the first time or revised as needed if the statement does exist. This is a critical step since every firm may have a slightly different view of the meaning of the value (e.g., what is the best definition of "integrity" or "putting customers first"?).

Our experience is that it is very beneficial for the working team to take a look at existing values and cultural statements from other organizations to see if their definition of the value can work or whether it needs to be adapted to better fit the organization. Simply put, the definitions have to "make sense" to employees in their particular organization and not just for organizations in general.

There are four key questions that the working team needs to ask themselves at this stage. First, is this the right preliminary list? Did the team miss any key value or cultural element even if it did not receive any votes in the workshop? Can this list be defended if challenged? Second, did we craft a simple, clear definition of every value and cultural element? Third, do the values (or cultural elements) work together to tell a story about our values (culture)? Fourth, do the values and culture support the mission, vision, and purpose? If we pass the screens of these four questions we are ready to test with key stakeholders.

Step 6: Test With a Variety of Key Stakeholders

There are three significant choices at this stage: (1) Who does one query and what is the sample of respondents in the organization? (2) What type of assessment do you conduct? (e.g., an online ranking of a preliminary list of values, or small workshops to assess and discuss the list), and (3) What is the approach that will be used to move from the preliminary list to the final list?

What is the sample of respondents? One suggestion is to sample all stakeholders who are significantly impacted by the values and culture. The minimum assessment would involve employees: their roles, functions, and levels within the organization. This is the most obvious group since they will experience the culture and values on a daily basis. Also, they will be asked to support and live the (revised) culture and values moving forward. Arguably, this assessment could be extended to partner organizations, the board, and/or key customers. However, depending on the nature of the organization, it should be considered an optional step.

What is the nature of the assessment that is conducted? There are an infinite number of ways to conduct this assessment. To make things simple, we would advocate for an approach that combines a quantitative analysis (simple scoring of the general assessments noted in Figs. 7.1 and 7.2 as well as the strongly agree/ strongly disagree scores of the criteria for both values and culture) with an opportunity to provide qualitative feedback. This feedback could take a variety of forms: town halls, workshops, focus groups, interviews, or other approaches. The important point is that the qualitative phase enables one to capture the rationale for the scoring, voices any concerns, and enables the working team to gain some insight on implementation.

How does one narrow down from a preliminary list to a final list? Certainly, one approach is to have individuals (either the working team or a broader sample) rank the order and/or prioritize the list through voting. The advantage of voting is that the results are very clear and the "cut-off" to accept a particular statement can be advocated in advance. The downside is that we observe that "the usual suspects" often rise to the top (e.g., teamwork). As noted earlier, if the usual suspects truly are selected, then the key is to use step 7 to define the statement in a way that fits the particular organization so that the definition can be customized. The principal disadvantage is that the minority point of view (e.g., a value statement was ranked lower) advocating for a lower-scoring item may not be heard. Thus, the narrowing exercise must allow for these "lower-ranked state-ments" to be advocated for in a larger forum. We have seen situations in which lower-ranked statements made the final list when the debate was taken seriously.

Step 7: Select, Refine, and Ratify Chosen Values and Culture

The working team at this stage works to refine, edit, and finalize the list of values and cultural elements. Again, this assumes we have the final list, and the task is to select exactly the right wording, keeping the statements short, and making it very easy to understand. After step 6, it is the task of the working team to create the final draft of the statements. This recommendation draft of values and cultural statements is presented to the steering team, which retains decision rights on the selection of values statements and cultural elements. It is often a good idea to have a working session with the steering team to get their input at this stage and then continue to refine.

A word of advice at this stage. Some will trivialize this stage, noting that it is simply wordsmithing of the final solution. However, that is not the case. The exact wording may take several (if not many) iterations to complete. The final version should not be rushed just to complete the task. It is perfectly fine for the working team to "set the draft aside" for a week or two. Once the final draft is handed to the steering committee, they will ratify the final versions.

Step 8: Rollout and Institutionalize

Similar to the MVP, the first step in the process is to build a communications rollout plan. This plan includes (1) details on the process that was followed by the working and steering teams, (2) the team composition (why these two groups?),

(3) the final list of the values and cultural statements, (4) specific commentary related to each statement as appropriate, and (5) the plan moving forward to embed the values and (revised) cultural elements across the entire organization.

The nonprofit firm had completed earlier work on leadership competencies. Hence, the rollout of the values and culture needed to take into account this recent workflow. As noted above, there was overlap between these elements. For example, putting their customers first was part of the leadership competency framework. At the same time, it was also noted as an organization value. Rather than be problematic, the organization saw this as inherently consistent with aligning values, leadership, and even strategy.

The mid-size technology firm conducted a rollout of the new values and cultural elements at the same time as the MVP. MVP was positioned as the guiding star that set the industry context and aspirations for the organization. The values and culture focused on the beliefs, norms, and desired behaviors that would help the organization realize its mission, vision, and purpose. This turned out to be fortuitous since all five choices—mission, vision, purpose, culture, and values—could be tightly aligned.

As the organization rolls out the culture and values, a contribution discussion is in order. Drucker believed that every single employee needed to support, reinforce, and live both the values and the culture. Similar to MVP, it is the individual's responsibility to align his/her behavior with the values and culture of the organization. Once again, the core belief is that self-control is the most powerful form of control: So, that is why you want the individual in the role to discuss with his/her boss how they can support the culture and values of the organization.

Conclusion

Every journey to revise (or build) a values statement and cultural elements is unique. However, the 8-step process described in this chapter is robust and can be employed at for-profits, nonprofits, and other organization forms. The most important step in this journey is the formulation of a strong, reliable, and high-performing working team. The strength of the working team will be an important signal to the organization about the importance of this effort. A second key point is to continually "test" the values and culture against the mission, vision, and purpose. Indeed, to go one step further, the values and culture must also support the strategy. In any rollout plan, this alignment must be made explicit (e.g., here is how our values support our mission).

Note

1. Halah Touryalai, "The Gospel of Wells Fargo," *Forbes*, January 25, 2012, https://www.forbes.com/sites/halahtouryalai/2012/01/25/the-gospel-according-to-wells-fargo/?sh=59eab1c07904

Chapter 8

Two Sources of Wisdom for Market Shapers, Peter Drucker and Confucianism

Introduction

Now that we have discussed each of the choices and how they collectively enhance each firms' creating the future efforts, we will provide a glimpse of the essential thinking that underlies our perspective in the first five chapters. No single chapter can do justice to Peter Drucker and the philosophy of Confucianism on these five core topics. Instead our aim is to provide a sampling of their insights related to each theme.

To begin, many firms would like to influence the market conditions in which they operate. Using today's business terminology, this would be a firm that does not accept the five forces of industry structure as a given – rather, they attempt to mold, influence, or shape industry evolution. However, most firms are passive and adapt to market trends.[1] Shaping the market is challenging, and even more so in this fast-changing VUCA (Volatility, Uncertainty, Complexity, and Ambiguity) time. Of course, there are various ways to think about shaping the market.[2] However, we believe that the Drucker and Confucian thinking behind our approach provide a unique perspective that complements more recent publications. Although the concepts we introduced in previous chapters are easy to understand, they are drawn from our long-term research on two classic and profound philosophies that are central to how organizations function: Peter Drucker's management theories and Confucianism.[3]

Peter Drucker (1909–2005) is regarded as the father of modern management who, according to many management theorists, "changed the face of industrial America."[4] Confucius (551–479 BC) is seen as the Socrates of China in the West,[5] a sage of Chinese literature and one of the most influential philosophers in Chinese history.

Creating the Organization of the Future, 75–100

Emerald Publishing Limited, Howard House, Wagon Lane, Bingley BD16 1WA, UK.

First published as 当德鲁克遇见孔夫子 (*"Setting the Direction for Your Firm"*) by Orient Publishing Center ("OPC"), with Bernard Jaworski and Virginia Cheung, China, 2021. English language translation copyright © 2023, Emerald Publishing Limited. This English language edition published under exclusive licence from OPC by Emerald Publishing Limited. Translated by Bernard Jaworski and Virginia Cheung. The moral right of the copyright holder and translator has been asserted. All rights of reproduction in any form reserved
doi:10.1108/978-1-83753-216-220231008

The names of Drucker and Confucius might come as a surprise to some readers. These two figures might be considered out of touch with today's modern realities. That reaction is understandable. In fact, people living in Confucian societies today often admit that it is challenging to understand Confucianism. The content is both challenging to comprehend and difficult to connect with the situations that many of us face in our modern working lives.

To the skeptics, though, we would say that studying the lessons of these two important figures actually offers an effective way for people to become empowered in the modern world, especially in the business world. Learning such lessons can help reveal opportunities hidden by uncertainties and turbulence that others cannot see. The selection of these two dominant thinkers represents an integration of ancient Oriental management philosophy and modern Western management. Given the long-term prosperity and rich theory development of both teachings, each contributes effective lessons that are timeless. In fact, it is often the case that world views can be limited by the cultures in which people live and the experiences they have had. This cultural view plays a more significant role in our daily behavior and decision-making process than we may realize, either consciously or unconsciously. In addition, our research found significant overlap and connection between these two time-tested philosophies.[6] As such, the essential concepts taken from these two philosophers provide a more holistic and integrated view for thinking about the market and guiding business practices, particularly in this period of deglobalization.

There are several significant similarities between the works of Drucker and Confucius that are helpful in supporting any firm's transformational journey to becoming a successful creator of the future. These similarities can be characterized in four ways.

First, both are people-focused. They are human-centered and concern themselves with people's values, growth, and development. Both are concerned with the essential spirit of human nature. Second, both are ultimately focused on a functioning society or social harmony. Drucker is described as "the man who invented management" and called himself a "social ecologist."[7] A functioning society was Drucker's main preoccupation throughout most of his work. Similarly, the ultimate goal of Confucianism is social harmony that aims for value-led social change through enhancing people's value systems and reshaping their behavior.[8] Third, Drucker's philosophy and Confucian principles are pragmatic and based on a broad array of transdisciplinary knowledge. Their work is clearly applicable and inspiring for practicing managers from different cultures. Drucker asserted that management is a liberal art, drawing on concepts from psychology, philosophy, history, and religion. The essence of management for him was "to make knowledge productive."[9] Confucianism, as a "philosophy of practical life,"[10] that has directed everyday life in China for more than a 1000 years. His work adapted other renowned Eastern philosophies like Taoism and Legalism, the writings of Mencius, and religions like Buddhism into a broader vision of Confucianism.[11]

Finally, although the five concepts of the framework discussed in this book's earlier chapters – compelling mission, vision, purpose, supporting values, and culture – can be traced to the work of Drucker and Confucius, it is a contemporary work that has been crafted by us to provide guidance to firms that want to create their futures. Market shaping is future-oriented and is the result of the decisions we make today. As Drucker noted, "effective managers should be able to manage both the present and the future."[12] We leverage these classic teachings as sources of wisdom that can be used to guide future growth.

To ensure that both legacies are practical, our approach has been designed to be a thinking guide that is managerially friendly and offers useful evaluative criteria for each of the five important choices. These criteria are also drawn from the core concepts of both philosophers to support effective implementation.

Mission

There are, of course, different ways to define a mission. For Drucker, it was clear that every organization needs a mission statement to articulate the underlying benefits desired by target customers rather than the product or technology (e.g., carmakers are in the transportation business, not the business of building cars). This explanation represents the fundamental customer focus and customer value-driven concepts of his management philosophy. Indeed, for Drucker, the mission must be customer value-driven, contribution-driven, and focused on strength.

External, Customer Value-Driven

A market is essentially formed by customer demand. One of Drucker's most widely recognized assertions is: "The only valid definition of business purpose is to create a customer."[13] Creating customers implies a new segment, and this requires firms to learn about each target customer segment wholeheartedly, identify the underlying value beyond product features, and design customized offerings that can deliver such value. This value can be a functional value, emotional value, symbolic value, and so on. The focus on mission is to understand chosen customer groups' unique desires, hopes, and needs.

For a B2C player such as Seasun Games, a game producer and distributor, their desired customer value is that their players discover the beauty in traditional Chinese fairy tale stories through their game and graphic designs. On the other hand, B2B firms need to consider both the customer and the consumer. For TCT, their desired value to the end consumer is to create safe and reliable rides for passengers. For direct customers – the metro companies that pay for their system – the desired value is not about the technology or system itself, but the reduced labor cost and user-friendly operation delivered by certain customized driverless functions.

Today's executives may be familiar with these concepts already. However even to some of the most thoughtful CEOs in the world, mission is not always an easy question to answer in practice. One of Drucker's most well-known consulting cases took place when Jack Welch became the new CEO of General Electric.

Drucker asked him: "If you weren't already in this business, would you still enter it today? If the answer is no, what are you going to do about it?"[14] It was this classic and profound question that inspired Welch to rethink his entire GE business portfolio. As a result of this set of choices as well as others, Welch successfully led GE to continue its high-performing run for the next 20 years.

These two criteria – external and customer focus – are important because traditional wisdom requires firms to position themselves within the market. This "positioning" mindset can often mislead firms to think from their own perspective and focus on what they can offer. Hence, the firm can become overly product- or technology-driven and lose the opportunity to shape the market. Instead, Drucker advocates that customized goods or services can "sell themselves." The goal is not to allocate resources on endless marketing campaigns that push customers by focusing on the "premier goods" or state-of-the-art technology per se. For Drucker, customers are neither standardized with the same need nor profit generators who will buy whatever existing products are offered by a firm. They need to be considered as differentiated individuals who should be served in particular contexts. For example, the same Micky Mouse from Disneyland needs to get adapted to different customs when he travels around the globe in order to provide localized stories for better communication with regional consumers.

Although there were no such concepts as a customer and customer value back in Confucius's time, Confucianism – like the Drucker philosophy – is also based in a focus on humanity. The Confucian virtue of benevolence, for example, represents "love and care" and the "extension of love and care" to each person in need. In a business context, we can understand the relationship between a firm and its customer in terms of the Confucian reciprocal "friend to friend" concept in the sense that the firm is willing to take care of a friend's specific needs, and customers appreciate this perceived value with a higher willingness to buy. This results in a value creation-based win-win relationship. Interestingly, as one of the earliest educators in China, Confucius was able to provide customized teaching for his "customers" (his students) by taking contextual conditions into consideration and providing customized solutions for his students,[15] unconsciously and without the knowledge of what would one day come to be known as "customer value." Confucius was a heavy promoter of the belief that you "do not give others what you don't want." Although this was a general principle and Confucius certainly wasn't thinking about customers when he said this, this idea does align with Drucker's notion of not becoming overly focused on what product and technology firms offer or have.

A clearly defined mission statement can help a firm to specify its target customers, which is a critical first step in deciding which market the firm wants to shape. Segmentation is a strategic choice that involves trade-offs. Here there is a risk for a mismatch between the desired customer value and the firm offering, thus negatively affecting customers' willingness to buy a product. A common issue faced by established firms is that trying to address too many segments thus resulting in spreading resources too thin. But Drucker's popular concept of "focusing on strength" means that it is the responsibility of the firm's executives to focus on the segment that best leverages the firm's strengths.

Internal, Contribution-Driven

While the mission is customer-centered, it's not just for customers. It's also a tool to align employees' contribution with customer value. It provides a direction toward effectiveness. It is mission alone, as Drucker stated, that "enables a business to set objectives, to develop strategies, to concentrate its resources, and to go to work. It alone enables a business to be managed for performance."[16]

After the firm decides on its desired customer value or benefits, it needs a team of like-minded individuals who understand the mission, believe in it, and live by it. Drucker believed that people are an organization's most important resources. Therefore, if the identified mission is inspiring and can resonate with the employees in a way that will engage everyone, then the process to realize the mission will both grow employees and align their contributions with the mission.

This is, however, an ongoing process that must be driven by executives – that, in fact, is a fundamental responsibility of leadership according to Drucker. But it cannot be accomplished by executives only. Rather, it's a collective effort involving everyone within the organization (all functions and ranks). This means that executives need to practice Drucker's principle of "pushing accountability down" by giving knowledge workers a sense of responsibility and ownership over the task – in particular, front-line employees – to drive any resolutions and determine how to best deliver the proposed customer value. For example, Southwest Airlines – which is highly recognized for its outstanding customer service – gives to its ground staff who are "closest to the event" the right to identify the best solutions to help passengers' urgent needs instead of asking managers for direction.

Drucker didn't aim to let executives choose between employees and customers. Rather, happy employees create happy customers. Firms can leverage their mission to bridge employee and customer value and to grow an organizational culture with higher staff engagement around how to deliver desired customer value. This also happens to be the practice of another Confucian principle, "establishing others as to establish yourself" – in other words, that employees become "established" through self-realization and satisfaction with their contributions. More importantly, these emotional gains are in addition to material gains and are often more lasting and fulfilling.

This Confucian principle of "establishing others as to establish yourself" can be seen as anticipating the concept of "customer orientation" which considers customers' needs and prioritizing customers' needs instead of one's own interests. In the previous example of Southwest Airlines, this means prioritizing passenger needs and not simply ignoring them just because they're not within your defined role. Southwest Airline's successful practice made them the carrier that received the fewest complaints of any US airline.[17] As their mission statement says: "Dedication to the highest quality of Customer Service delivered with a sense of warmth, friendliness, individual pride, and Company Spirit."[18] This statement reflects the core ideas behind the "happy employees create happy customers" story.

Managing Continuity and Change

For firms aiming to create the future, it might be common wisdom to say they must be aware that whenever the market they're in changes, they should reconsider their mission to fit current events and market trends. This is a well-known concept of Drucker's – his "theory of the business."[19]

Drucker believed that every organization needs a valid theory of business in order for its executives to be able to address one of the most important and strategic issues – "what to do and what *not* to do." It is not an easy decision, and firms need a set of supporting marketing activities that generate, share, and make use of intelligence.[20] These are challenging tasks, but they are crucial to becoming market-oriented.

"What to do" implies "what the firm gets paid for" – but the reality is, today's customer is being trained by the marketplace to desire constant innovation. Despite the fact that customer value can change overnight, it takes time for firms to switch their businesses. Market conditions may change radically month after month, but any firm needs stable performance. This dilemma is supported by Drucker's concept regarding managing continuity and change – to manage both the present and future.[21] He argued, managers must be prepared to accept that the right business today may not be the same in the long term. That's because the root cause of many business problems is not doing the wrong things but doing the right things that don't fit the present reality.[22] Confucianism "agrees" with the idea of constant change and that further proposed change is not absolute but depends on context.[23] The Confucian approach also considers context and reinterpretation[24] – which carry the same essence as the theory of business. Therefore, the competence to navigate continuity and change is the key to any firm's sustainability. It also suggests that, even for firms with a compelling mission, it's still crucial to diagnose if the firm can continue to provide the right customer value on a regular basis.

As mentioned earlier, many people today regard a classic text (like those by Confucius or Peter Drucker) as signifying an old tradition that is obsolete – that our world is too technically advanced to require any references from the past. A 1000 years ago, however, Confucius already was challenging this bias. He recognized the importance and necessity of historical data, and he required people to learn from the past, classic texts, and other experiences in order to create a base for envisioning a better future and growth. He noted that one cannot be future-oriented based on ignorance of the past. Of course, his goal in learning from the past was not aimed at a better understanding of markets or customers but was directed at the level of his society and bringing about value-led social change.[25] Similarly, to bridge the gap between learning from the past and creating the future, Drucker's principle of "balancing short-term and long-term goals" offers theoretical support for a smooth transition across different time periods, and that is critical for firms to think about as they consider their missions.

In these difficult VUCA and post-COVID-19 times, firms suffering from decreasing revenue in core markets are actively looking for new business opportunities. It's understandable that it is very attractive to pursue business diversification, but our observation is that many firms make too easy a decision to change their existing business without sufficient analysis in response to the question, "what business should we be in?" This "what is right" question can be complex as it involves balancing value creation for different stakeholders – customer value (mission), for example, or social value (purpose) – and often this requires a good combination of both. Patagonia's mission to "save our home planet" is a good example of striking the balance between doing well and doing good – taking care of the environment while providing the right value to customers through high quality and durable outdoor wear.[26] Thus, to define mission and purpose can be an effective start to balancing continuity and change by leading a firm to make the right choice about tomorrow's business.

Drucker noted that a good mission statement should articulate a firm's competitive advantage to its target customers. Once again, to make a choice between different customer value requires a "focus on strength." A common mistake in defining a valid mission statement is forgetting that it must be based on real strengths – not on aspirations or hoped-for strengths. Our observation is that it's not atypical that executives have personal bias about their firms' core strengths, assets, and capabilities.

Consider the example of Kodak. Despite many explanations about Kodak's decline, the common view is that the company didn't recognize the inevitable trend in the industry toward digitization. In fact, Kodak did know that digital technology would eventually dominate the market, and it invested in being a pioneer in this area. The very first digital camera was invented by Kodak in 1975.[27] But Kodak's blind faith in customer value took priority over technology issues. When Kodak recognized changing customer behaviors – that people were starting to share pictures on social media rather than printing them out at local retailers – the company acquired Ofoto (a photo-sharing site) in 2001, which was well ahead of the creation of Meta (Facebook).[28] But Kodak mistakenly assumed that its core customer value was in *saving* memorable moments, not *sharing* them, and Ofoto was used only as an extension of selling film, which was still Kodak's core business at the time. Just imagine if Kodak had recognized the potential impact of emerging online social communities: Kodak would be a very different company today.

Mission is a management tool for responding to continuity and change, but to work effectively, it needs to be simple enough – like the slogan on a T-shirt – for people to remember. It's easier for a firm to develop a list of 20 or 30 assumptions about market trends than to choose just three or four key trends that can create the most significant impact on its target market. It may sound simple, but it is in fact drawn from Drucker's principle of "regular abandonment" and a "focus on strength."

Vision

Vision depicts a firm's ideal end state – that is, a "common dream" uniquely belonging to that firm. Even when there are two players in the same industry with seemingly identical offerings, such as Space X and Blue Origin, their distinct destinations put them on different paths and results in different performances. Elon Musk's dream for Space X is multiplanetary – carrying humans to Mars or other planets to live there,[29] whereas Jeff Bezos's wish is to remove all damaging activities to other planets in order to preserve Earth.[30] Bezos wants a better Earth by building a path to space, and then returning to Earth as the final destination, while Musk's destination is Mars and beyond.

For executives aiming to be market shapers, having a vision is the first step in a firm's transformational journey. In Drucker's words: "Goals can be set. And performance can be measured. And then business can perform."[31] By the same token, Confucius also pointed out the importance of goal setting, which decides the direction of an action plan. Musk and Bezos publicly announced how they envisioned the industry and the future of humans and Earth, and each attracts followers who share their dreams. Therefore, visionary firms must first articulate their unique point of view about the market that they want to shape.

Grow Through Distinctive Challenges

Since Drucker first developed the concept of the knowledge worker, it has moved to center stage and now plays a dominant role in today's organizations. Knowledge workers with critical thinking and independent judgment often have a clear view of their own visions, which are best for them and not necessarily for others. Further, these creative talents are often curious and continual learners with diversified and ever-evolving interests. That is why it's more challenging for a single vision to adequately address the interest of the firm's majority, if not everyone. In the famous parable of the three bricklayers who are building a cathedral, each is performing the same work with different ideal end states in their hearts and minds. In the past, we might have assumed that the goal of creating a cathedral would be a motivating vision for all three. But the parable shows us that one bricklayer is satisfied with just laying the bricks, while the other two have larger, grander interpretations for their actions. Creating a vision that is "fit" to today's diversified organizations is critical. If we borrow from that parable and apply it to management, the envisioned cathedral should lead to a heaven to which everyone wants to go, not just for some.

As younger generations of workers are experiencing more choices in life, financial rewards are becoming less motivating. These younger workers tend to resonate more with a subject or a thing or an idea – in other words, with a vision itself. In fact, young and well-educated employees are more likely to be attracted by a like-minded team working on a challenge that can have some positive impact on the world. Having these workers feel proud to be part of an activity is highly motivating.

Both Drucker and Confucius place a strong emphasis on self-management and individual growth. Most younger employees today understand that continual learning is a source of competitive advantage. As such, they frequently embrace new challenges and avoid repetitive work. From a learning perspective, then, a challenging vision can be very inspiring – which is related to Drucker's view of growing people through challenges. As an undeniable market shaper, Apple is an excellent example of a company that motivates employees with a challenging vision "to make the best products on earth, and to leave the world better than we found it."[32] That vision is a call to action for ambitious talent, for them to have the chance to work with some of the world's best engineers to create global influence together. This vision depicts a unique learning opportunity for its people.

Another aspect of this challenge-based motivation is to be distinct from one's competitors, which Confucius stated a 1000 years ago as "making the journey one's own."[33] Steve Jobs, for example, shaped a culture of excellence at Apple that depicted the world in stark terms as a place consisting of "Apple" and "non-Apple" – not Apple versus Microsoft or any other competitors. As a result, we can see many talented professionals across the globe wanting to join Apple to embrace a vision that they may not find at other Silicon Valley firms. The Apple vision is obviously not designed for everyone.

Vision is the North Star that guides decisions, and Drucker's classic question "what to abandon?" offers a test of that vision. As he once asked: "If we did not already do this, would we go into it now?" To offer another example, the vision of the Chinese tech company TCT is "to become a world-class technical leader"[34] This vision provides a clear view of where to focus and how to decide on its resource distribution. In TCT's case, the firm must prioritize continuous investment in R&D to enhance its core competence in both good and bad years.

Given that both Drucker and Confucianism are pragmatic and results-driven, a company's vision has to be challenging yet achievable for employees to take it seriously. We have observed that, in China, many similar visions across all sectors center on the goal "to become a global leader" in their fields. In TCT's case, the team also had the incentive "to become a global leader in rail transit." However, this ambitious goal requires much more than just making state-of-the-art products. It's neither necessary nor possible for every firm to be a leader in every respect. After taking time to think about business reality, achievable goals, and how to play to their strengths (as Drucker suggested), the TCT team concluded for now that they only had the research capability to win on technical innovations globally. This kind of open, honest, and complete disclosure of challenges and strength not only helped to draft a vision that fit TCT but also the whole team benefited from having this discussion.

In practice, for most of the firms in this world, persistence and grit are key success factors. A firm with an inspiring and challenging vision signals to its team that there's a long and tough way ahead. And when the team is on the verge of giving up, that vision serves to help guide their direction. The vision provides hope to overcome difficulties and helps drive the company's workforce to achieve as much as possible. Similarly, as Confucius stated, "When it is obvious that the goals cannot be reached, don't adjust the goals, adjust the action steps." A strong vision ensures a first step to begin that long and transformative journey.

Use Visual Communication

Vision statements – as a formal communication to both employees and external stakeholders – have to be easy to comprehend for effective communication with a broad, diversified audience.

Internally, a vision is used to align everyone's understanding about the ideal end state. This is important because every knowledge worker can have a different understanding of the same statement because everyone is influenced differently by the culture around them or by the personal experiences and perspectives that they bring to the situation. Thus, image-based language can often be a useful way to communicate to all of the audiences in a cross-culture setting. In the parable of the three bricklayers building a cathedral, the cathedral provides a simple, universal image that everyone can easily imagine.

When dealing with the question of vision, it's also important to remember that vision is future-oriented and very similar to the "unfelt want" concept of Drucker – that it describes a need beyond customers' current expectations (think of the impact of the smartphone when it was first introduced to consumers) and that the customers don't realize they need until they see it. That is why firms need to prepare their very own "crystal ball" to visualize the future and communicate it to their audiences. This is particularly true of customers and the general public who may not have any previous knowledge of that industry and its technology. In the example of TCT, its vision "to create better life with mobility" is concise, and people can easily imagine this desired end state – a convenient life thanks to mobility. This is in sharp contrast to being stuck in traffic. Instead one can enjoy a worry-free ride with a safe, fast, and comfortable point-to-point metro service. The vision could even include customized solutions as the firm depicts their next generation of metro to us. Here passengers can reserve with a mobile app an airport express with a gym facility or a meeting room on the train. Such simple statements are an effective mode of communication to customers, providing a "visualized future" that allows customers to better understand how this vision relates to their individual needs.

As Drucker repeatedly emphasized the importance of the "value customers can perceive," drafting a vision statement should involve considering how the customer feels when the vision is achieved. Alibaba, the well-known Chinese e-commerce giant, uses vivid imagery in their mission/vision statement: "We aim to build the future infrastructure of commerce. We envision that our customers will meet, work and live at Alibaba, and that we will be a company that lasts at least 102 years."[35] This statement clearly focuses on customers even though it would be difficult for most customers to imagine what value they will receive from living and working at Alibaba for 102 years!

A powerful vision statement serves as any firm's public commitment to its future performance and what that future will look like when it has achieved its mission. This is very consistent with Drucker's famous comment that "The best way to predict the future is to create it." The end-state contained within your vision statement is the future that you want to create with your firm in the market.

Purpose

Successful executives seldom have the luxury to sit back and ponder why their firms exist. The answer might seem obvious – that, as Milton Friedman noted, the only duty of the firm is to maximize profits for its stockholders.[36] But even for a firm that is struggling to survive, that question of existence or having social impact rarely comes up. The existence and operation of any firm consumes social resources, and we must consider what this means in terms of a firm's social value.

Though Peter Drucker didn't make a clear distinction between customer value (mission) and social value (purpose), we feel the need to differentiate here because purpose is a key factor in supporting any firm's sustainability. Firms need a sense of purpose in order to think of the common good rather than just profit maximization. Why is this necessary? For any firm that wants to become a creator of the future, the market has to be broadly defined to include not only various stakeholders but society as a whole. When firms are seen as organs of the society in which they exist, they have a responsibility to produce a positive impact for on that society's sustainability – something that Drucker called a "functioning society" while Confucius used "harmonious" to describe the ultimate goal.

Both Drucker and Confucius focus on the vital necessity of social good in their works. Despite being separated by thousands of years, they share many similar characteristics: They are likeminded, believe in the "natural kindness" of people, and care about society. Thus, firms that adopt these qualities and have clearly defined purpose statements that show a commitment to society can actually become powerful motivations for employees, customers, and other stakeholders in their community.

Drucker and Confucius's visions of social impact are finding receptive audiences today, especially among younger workers with a strong desire for purpose in their professional and personal lives. Many firms are experiencing an increasing desire from their employees for work that gives them a sense of meaning, not just a paycheck. One surprising statistic indicates that 90% of employees are actually willing to earn less in order to work with a purpose, and 80% of CEOs agree on the need to balance company profits with a sense of purpose for their workforce.[37]

This is especially noticeable in the area of consumer goods, and any brand's position regarding green and sustainability issues influences consumers' purchasing decisions more than ever before[38] with 63% preferring purpose-driven brands. Many brands have found ways to embed social value in their core identities; these include Starbucks, Apple, Tesla, Ikea, Disney, Johnson & Johnson, and Patagonia, which all perform well in the market.[39] This suggests why purpose statements can be very powerful and why some of the most visionary firms have them.[40]

Align Individual Purpose and Organizational Purpose

Many firms are struggling to keep their teams motivated, and even some of the world's best companies (like Apple) have had trouble getting employees to return to the office since the start of the pandemic.[41] Staff motivation has always been an important topic for many firms, though not for the top-ranked ones that have assumed they can always attract quality talent with competitive compensation packages. This still seems to be the case for many Chinese firms across diversified industries; new graduates today are requiring more financial reassurances given that we are in an economic downturn. But Peter Drucker and others have challenged the profit motive and have argued that it isn't the only decisive factor in how people choose their careers (or at least it's not the primary one).[42] Considering that high-quality talents are working as volunteers for nonprofits or as social workers, there must be some other valid reasons why they are willingly choosing low pay or no pay at all.

Drucker and Confucius recognized that every person has a desire to contribute in a purposeful way to society. A limited number of firms recognize this increasing calling, and even fewer know how to respond. For those employees who don't feel a sense of purpose, another activity might be considered a "better use of time" – for example, spending time with family and friends, or taking another job. According to a McKinsey report, about 70% of people define their personal purpose through their work, and millennials are even more likely to see their work as a life calling. As a result of the global pandemic, 70% of employees have been reflecting on their purpose, and half of US employees are reconsidering the work they want to do.[43] Financial stability certainly remains an important factor in how many people choose careers, but a sense of purpose and other related qualities – like autonomy and freedom – are becoming increasingly important factors, too.

Although drafting a purpose statement is the work must be driven by the executive team, this should be a collective and ongoing process that requires the engagement of employees at all levels, allowing everyone to define how their own duties align with the firm's overall purpose. Drucker noted that everyone in a knowledge organization "must think through their objectives and their contributions and take responsibility for both …regardless of his or her particular job."[44]

In the case of TCT, their desired social value is to foster technical innovation, and that is why a heavy investment in R&D is intended to promote rates of innovation rather than slow down the competition. When, for example, TCT realized a significant breakthrough with driverless trains,[45] their entire team – from managers to staff – was excited. One frontline employee described his pride when he brought his son to see the first driverless train that was produced by a team in which he'd participated. We could feel his excitement as he shared his feelings, and it demonstrated for us the inspirational power that is created when people share in a greater dream.

Drucker defined an organization as being "the place to convert knowledge workers' specialized knowledge into performance, to make them effective."[46] Firms have a responsibility to professionally develop their employees, but helping them gain a sense of purpose is a new exercise for many with about 85% feeling they have a purpose and only about 65% believing that they can actually articulate what that purpose is.[47] Thus it is necessary for firms to learn not just how to shape a clearly defined, well-summarized purpose statement in collaboration with their employees but also to help them to align their individual purposes with the organization's.

Purpose needs to be motivational; employees want to be accountable and responsible. This applies not just in the US and the West, but also in Confucian societies – despite the stereotypes that say people in such societies are less interested in individual purpose because it is more socially desirable to sacrifice individual goals for the greater good. It is certainly true that Eastern philosophies often stress collectivism to a degree that is not found in a Western working environment. In traditional Confucian society, it is assumed that well-trained superior individuals ("junzi") will leverage their knowledge to better manage their families, country, and ultimately contribute to a harmonious society.[48] If a conflict arises between the common good and an individual's self-interest, self-sacrifice is expected. Such behavior might be diminishing today, but this mindset is still influential enough in many workplaces – often unconsciously – that it is critical for firms in Confucian societies to clearly articulate their purpose. If the firm doesn't have a credible and motivating purpose connected with a good cause, employees may question the legitimacy and value of their "self-sacrifice." Take the "996" working culture of Alibaba as another example.[49] A model that requires employees to work from 9 a.m. to 9 p.m., six days a week, it received severe criticism after several *karoshi* cases (occupation-related sudden death) and a soaring turnover rate, and the situation was exacerbated by a statement from Alibaba's founder, Jack Ma, who said that "employees who get the 'opportunity' to work a 996 schedule are the 'lucky' ones." Many of the company's hard-working employees were disappointed by Ma's statement, which seemed to diminish the purpose of their sacrifices.

Having a well-defined purpose produces many obvious benefits. Many studies show that employees who feel purposeful at work are six times more likely to want to stay at the company, and 1.5 times more likely to go above and beyond to make their company successful.[50]

Do Well by Doing Good

To create an inspiring sense of purpose at work, a firm's purpose statement must clearly articulate how its desired social impact is connected with its daily operations and how this impact can be delivered through its products and services. This connecting-the-dots process is part of bridging a firm's specific offerings and operations to its societal outcomes. Firms may prefer to focus on their missions instead because this is easier and customer value is more directly connected to a willingness to buy with an immediate cash return; on the other hand, focusing on a firm's social value may suggest a contribution that is going to cost the firm in some economic way and lead to financial loss. In fact, if any firm can connect the dots on its social value, this can become a unique source of competitive advantage. That is what Drucker distinctively suggested – "do well by doing good" – by turning social problems into profitable business opportunities. Tesla is a good example because of its core value of "environmental consciousness"[51] that has helped the company to gain brand recognition and a high public relations profile. A message that is environmentally conscious makes consumers believe that their purchases of this innovative technology are serving the environment and the common good (or at least not causing extra harm). This noble sense of value has gained Tesla greater customer loyalty and better retention of its market share, which translates into impressive financial gains.

Today Drucker's vision of increasing the number of socially responsible organizations[52] is becoming a reality. Drucker introduced this idea at a time when organizations weren't aware of their reciprocal relationship with society. His assertion was a strong response to the opposing argument that socially responsible activities can hurt profitability, and it emphasized that corporate social responsibility (CSR) shouldn't be narrowly defined just in terms of philanthropy. That message isn't just important to internal employees but also to external stakeholders. When customers understand how a product is associated with social impact, it influences their purchase decisions.

Drucker's "do well by doing good" sets a high standard for firms. It requires that firms focus on eliminating any harmful, negative byproducts of their production and operation processes. Today, not all firms across the globe have realized this duty as a part of their purpose. But some, like Starbucks, stopped providing plastic straws years ago in an effort to help lessen pollution, and they are not the only ones. Countless other companies such as Patagonia, All Good Products, and Warby Parker,[53] which enjoy good profits, still exercise a measure of social responsibility.

The vital importance of purpose doesn't apply only to B2C players; it must also play a part in B2B firms. We can see this, for example, in the construction industry, in which businesses traditionally compete against each other and receive increasing criticism for working conditions and pollution. China State Construction Engineering Corporation (CSEC) has promoted its use of steel in its projects. This decision may be more expensive than what its competitors are doing, but it provides a more optimized solution than using traditional concrete, which may be cheaper than steel but results in more waste and a negative societal impact.

Although profit-making, values, and social contributions are not necessarily contradictory choices, Drucker reminded us that a firm's purpose should not exceed its limit of resources and legitimacy, which he described using the term "bounded goodness." In practice, not all firms can aim for global impact as illustrated by Siemens and Microsoft in previous chapters. A local convenience store located on a corner in Los Angeles or Kansas City might have a very modest social impact: its purpose statement (if it has one) might be simply to satisfy the urgent needs of its surrounding community with 24/7 service. But when that little store belongs to something larger like, say, 7-Eleven, as a multinational player this company aims for much greater impact and serves more people across the globe with the quality of its standardized goods and services.

The Confucian principle of "establishing others as to establish yourself" requires virtuous people to help others as they help themselves. In addition to performing their own duties in their roles, this principle is similar to Drucker's assertion that a firm should bear responsibility in facing social problems not caused by the firm, in addition to eliminating any negative results that it might directly cause *to* society. Despite the common misunderstanding that Confucianism is "opposed to profit-making,"[54] Confucius did suggest that people who only think about maximizing personal profit without considering the overall prosperity of their community should be disdained and excluded. His words anticipate many companies that have failed and didn't appear to embrace the importance of understanding their purpose. OFO, a fast-growing (and fast-disappearing) bicycle-sharing company that was once valued at $3 billion, became a unicorn in just a few years.[55] That firm blindly focused on growing ridership only and ignored the countless broken bikes discarded on the streets that resulted in numerous social costs and inconveniences for others. Indeed, if all firms would practice the Confucian virtue of righteousness and become equally purpose-driven, there would be less issues involving free riders on public goods as in the case of OFO.

Of course, purpose must be firm-specific, and Drucker suggested that visionary executives should not focus only on financials but consider positive social impact such as professional development for their staff and helping them grow. These elements of the common good are normally valued by various stakeholders[56] and can be a good place to start connecting the dots by making employees feel proud to be part of the company.

Values

"Organizations have to have values,"[57] Drucker wrote, explaining that, without a strong commitment to shared values, there is no enterprise.[58] Similarly, Confucianism shares an equal focus on values as illustrated by this saying: "The superior man thinks always of virtue; the common man[59] thinks of comfort."[60] Although this statement is addressed on the individual level (because there was no such concept of the organization in his time), it is still very clear that values matter to both individuals and organizations.

Today many firms recognize that values are important, and their value statements are presented in bold headlines on their homepages and office walls. Unfortunately, that's all that most do with their value statements. Drucker and Confucius believed that values may vary, but once these values are stated, everyone must buy into them and live by them. Values are as essential to how organizations and society function "as a human body needs vitamins and minerals,"[61] Drucker wrote. In an ideal situation, shared values form a common belief, and value-led behaviors should become the norm for directing people's daily behavior. Confucius described values as a directional North Star for leaders, stating: "One who rules through the power of virtue is analogous to the polestar: it simply remains in its place and receives the homage of the myriad lesser stars."[62]

Theoretically, a communal ritual's strong symbolic effect should make it a powerful managerial tool for bringing people together as a team. But enforcing one fixed set of values is often very difficult to do. It's not unusual, in fact, to hear criticisms from Generation Z about what are called "organizational rituals." That's because there's simply no value, norm, rule, or belief that can be widely agreed upon by every individual employee and strictly followed in daily operation. To many employees, these rituals are seen just as unnecessary burdens.

This issue raises a serious question about managerial effectiveness and the importance of standardization: Is it still legitimate and necessary to have a unified set of values? Drucker suggested that, although one's personal values may not be exactly the same as an organization's values, they should be at least "compatible for one to be effective to produce results."[63] Values fit is the precondition for employees to live with the firm's values.

Define Actionable Values to Inform Decisions

Values are the guardrail of decision-making; therefore, effective implementation requires that a value statement must be simple enough for employees to translate into practical behaviors. For example, some of the most common values shared by Fortune 500 companies include "care (service, compassion)" and "teamwork (collaboration, cooperation),"[64] but how do we understand the practice of care and teamwork for a specific firm? Confucianism was already advocating for the virtue of benevolence thousands of years ago, but it's a natural tendency for people now to prioritize their own tasks before being cooperative and helping out coworkers.

At Tesla, their core values comprise "doing the best, taking risks, respect, constant learning, and environmental consciousness." These are meaningful values that can inform decisions and support Tesla's effort to become the leading player for a good cause (environmental consciousness). These are also easy to understand and can be accomplished with continual learning and technical innovation.

Not every company will have an experience like Tesla's. For some, values are often treated as vague concepts, and when this involves an established multinational with a very diversified workforce, vague values will be interpreted and understood in completely different ways according to the communities and cultures in which these employees live. Take the value of teamwork. Teamwork is a universal value that most organizations embrace, but everyone doesn't understand it in the same way. Workers in Confucian societies may understand teamwork as meaning "do not speak up" in order to maintain a harmonious relationship in the office or with clients. In the Silicon Valley, however, constructive confrontation may be accepted or even encouraged as a cooperative way of communicating to help the team be effective.

Another difference is that not all values will be equally meaningful to all stakeholders across different time periods. For example, to align the seemingly common shared value of "integrity" became a two-way selection and matching process between stakeholders of Vanke, a property development firm. Its shareholders, employees, and customers all had different understandings about the meaning of the firm's "no bribery offering" policy.[65] Although Drucker and

Confucius advocate virtuous practices before profit maximization, this value resulted in a loss of Vanke's shareholders' short-term profits because of a higher cost for land. However, in the longer term, as this value started to gain more brand recognition among consumers, more business partners with the same value were attracted to work with Vanke, which became regarded as a "trusted brand."

Thus, meaningful and understandable values must be the North Star that guides an organization so that it follows values-led conduct. As Drucker asserted, once an organization has clearly defined its values, it should "refrain from tackling tasks that do not fit into its value system." If it doesn't, he warned, "as a result, it will do damage rather than good." This process can take time. If a firm has high-performing employees who disagree with the firm's values, Drucker suggests that values can serve as "the ultimate test" of who belongs with the company and that value-led individuals should be given positions as role models for other employees. As a result, organizations can leverage clearly defined value statements as a powerful tool for hiring and evaluation. This may sound unfair and may lead to the short-term losses of some good employees, but it makes more sense when we consider a longer time frame. If an employee's strengths do not fit with their firm's value system, this job may still not be the one "to devote his/her life in"[66] even if they are performing well in their current role. Drucker understood this situation in very personal terms. Even though he had talents and abilities as a high-performing bank employee, this career was not the perfect value fit for him.[67]

Consider Cultural Differences in Making Choices About Values

As mentioned earlier, there are indeed some universal values that are highly credited in any culture across the globe and that are applicable in any industry. These are "must have" values such as integrity, trust, honesty, and so on. There are also many culture-specific, industry-specific, and firm-specific values. For international conglomerates, they can apply general universal values at the group level and localize these values when applying them in regions and specific business units. However, in the business world, we observe that values can be connected to different behaviors and job expectations in cross-culture settings, and it's not unusual for international players to have difficulties understanding some of their employees, customers, and suppliers because these groups live and work in a culture that they don't understand.

Budweiser presents a clear example of these cultural differences. When Budweiser's responsible drinking value[68] encountered the traditional "drink till you drop" culture in China, the company launched product lines and smaller bottles specifically connected to responsible drinking behavior. The company also focused on beverages with less alcohol content in order to target younger health-conscious consumers in that culture.

In the eyes of Drucker and Confucius, certain socially important values involving "community," "environment," "learning," "people," and "responsibility" on a personal level are common "must have" values. Once again, however, even "must have" values are open to some interpretation. Consider, for example, how responsibility is understood by Huawei, a leading Chinese telecom powerhouse. Huawei incorporates founder Ren Zhengfei's personal experiences and uses military terms to explain accountability and commitment in terms of the need to "strive" and exhibit a "wolf spirit."[69] Employees are expected to overwork, aiming high and striving to climb up the social ladder. Everyone in the company shares an attitude of being "ready to go to the battlefield" at any given time and behaviors like sleeping on a mattress in the office.[70] Although these values and expectations may have a significant influence on many Chinese firms and be treated as popular management mantras, it isn't clear that they will continue to resonate with younger generations of workers (not to mention with employees from different cultures) who aren't accustomed to viewing work in militaristic terms.

If we consider the cultural context of firm-specific values, the most widely accepted values in Confucian societies are the "Five Virtues" – benevolence (*ren*), righteousness (*yi*), ritual (*li*), wisdom (*zhi*), and trust (*xin*).[71] These values may seem difficult to connect with modern professional life, but a value like wisdom actually has much in common with Drucker's "continuous learning." Based on our observations of the current business landscape, though, the emphasis placed on learning in many Chinese organizations actually relates to the higher requirement of employees' degrees rather than to investment in their learning and training on job.

As both Drucker and Confucian teachings suggest, the mind should be guided by virtuous thinking[72] and should be results-driven. That being said, firms should leverage their values in making value-led decisions and translating performance using evaluation systems like KPI or OKR to ensure that direct results can be measured.

Values Fit

For conceptual values to be useful and make a real difference in a firm's performance, they should be able to support the firm's strategy in a specific way. Values fit is a compelling Drucker principle used to balance short-term and long-term strategies. Managers, Drucker explained, "have to base their decisions on what is right rather than on what is acceptable."[73]

A successful example of that is Michelin, which is a global leader in mobility. With a core strategy of "sustainable mobility," the company's key value of respect is defined according to this strategy: in other words, respect for customers is demonstrated through innovation and respect for the environment through sustainable development.[74] Thoughtful values guide Michelin's specific behavior to innovate with sustainable high-tech materials in support of its strategy.

Clearly defined values provide the reasoning and motivations to support firms in their decisions about strategy and conduct. But making "values fit" choices may involve tradeoffs, as there are always strong temptations to pursue short-term opportunities or harmful behavior because it will be profitable. The food company Kraft Heinz, for example, has core values that comprise "customer first, innovation, integrity, ownership, quality."[75] Whereas integrity and quality fall into the noble category of Confucius, these two values are also very high level and general: they don't provide any specific product strategies necessary for the company to be a "responsible producer." Instead, we find increasing criticism that products like their signature ketchup could be unhealthy to consume over time.[76] If true, it would not align with their values – even though it would certainly be a profitable product for the company. This example demonstrates why firms must consider balancing long-term and short-term strategies to make a public commitment based on values.

Culture

Culture might be the most familiar concept to many, but there are many diverging definitions and understandings about what culture means. Culture demonstrates "how we work here" – in other words, it refers to the unspoken consensus regarding how you practice and perform at work, akin to the concept of rituals in Confucianism. From our viewpoint, shaping a strong culture involves a process of translating conceptual values into explicit cultural behaviors. It doesn't matter how strong a firm's strategic plan is, From a Drucker's perspective, a firm's strategy will not succeed unless it supported by a strong culture. Theoretically, if the firm aligns all of these elements – vision, mission, purpose, values, and culture – it is more likely to have an impact on creating the future.

Values decide the direction of a cultural action plan. Whether the desired cultural behavior is big or small, shaping a culture needs to be learned and repeated on a regular basis. This process takes time, resources, and persistent effort. Although culture is not a panacea for solving all management woes, a good culture can improve all aspects of how employees think and behave within their organizations. Further, we have found in our empirical study of Chinese firms that the role model effect of a firm's executives can be a significant motivational factor along with changing social desirability that play an influential role in shaping value-led behaviors, especially among younger employees.

Define "Fit"

A strong culture can be a source of comparative advantage, as both Drucker and Confucius suggested. By focusing on strengths and the current context, firms aiming to shape markets must have a unique culture that "fits their shaping strategy" rather than just being perceived as popular.

Today every organization has its own corporate culture, and our empirical studies show that many firms in developing countries like China strongly promote the value of "striving" and the behavior of "overtime," which could become a barrier in hiring some staff. However, if such values can be interpreted correctly as expressions of effectiveness and being results-driven, "overtime" is in fact an effective cultural behavior to support the value of "striving" to achieve the desired goal. Apple's culture of excellence is definitely not a fit for everyone, but this has never become a barrier for them; rather, it has resulted in the creation of a culture that attracts the right talent. That is because the idea that one must "strive to be excellent" is a motivational and aspirational form of culture that will attract the best of the best, and those are the kinds of people that Apple wants. What's particularly interesting is that this approach is embedded organization-wide, from hiring and evaluation to product design and the selection of vendors and suppliers. Thus a clear and unique choice of culture creates the best matching between the organization and its employees as well as partners. It becomes a filter that helps to enhance the firm's comparative advantage, similar to Netflix's sports team culture (which is not for everyone, either).

Culture is a very complex concept, and most firms have features and values that would probably fit well into many different types of cultures. When Drucker said that it was important to "employ the whole man," he was acknowledging this complexity – that an organization as a whole will have comprehensive needs and often there are cultural elements that are seemingly in conflict with each other. TCT values both safety and innovation as *sine qua non* elements of corporate culture compared with other companies in the railway industry that favor more traditional ideas and practices such as keeping the system stable and minimizing any changes to match critical safety requirements. This seems to suggest that innovation is somehow in conflict with safety, but it isn't. In fact, TCT realized that its unique culture was to leverage its capability in independent innovation to deliver a system with a higher level of safety. This example suggests how drafting a good cultural statement may not only helps the firm to identify points of tension between cultural elements but also it will learn how to balance them, which translates into a unique competitive advantage.

There are some cases where this kind of resolution between apparently conflicting elements doesn't happen. There are some elements in business that are unable to coexist, and in those cases, the firm is forced to make a bet. For example, a common desirable cultural element among many young people today is the attainment of happiness, which they believe the workplace must provide. The fact is, no job can keep employees happy all of the time, and close study of various firms shows that innovation actually often comes from frustration.[77] Thus, a thorough discussion about a firm's desired culture also involves helping employees to understand what they truly want from their work. There are trade-offs in such strategic choices, and it is up to employees to supply their own answers.

There is no single best culture, and firms have to make specific bets on what is a "fit" for them. Some multinationals need to maintain a robust hierarchical structure to deliver standardized products and services across the globe (think McDonald's or General Motors[78]); other firms like W. L. Gore & Associates – recognized as the "Best Workplace" by *Fortune* consecutively[79] – choose a delayered structure to build a people-focused and trust-based family culture. In fact, the society in which the firm operates and its associated social desirability often have strong influences on the firm's choice of culture. For example, in contrast to Apple and Netflix's choices of a competitive sports team culture, many managers in China and Japan naturally prefer benevolence and family culture – and as such view their organizations as extended families. In contrast to Microsoft's choice of constructive confrontation in meetings, many employees in China possess a natural expectation that they will assume a harmonious relationship with their peers and receive selfless support from their managers. They regard these elements as a must, and they would become disappointed if they didn't receive it. This so-called "new kids at work" phenomenon is becoming common among Millennials and Generation Z across the globe.[80] As of today, firms practicing Drucker's principle of "regular abandonment"[81] understand that they need to review their bets according to changes in context. A good example of that is the Chinese construction company Shenzhen Decoration, which redefined and shifted its culture from "family" to "productive family" in order to focus on effectiveness and putting an emphasis on being results-driven.

We find ourselves in a fast-changing business environment today: knowledge changes quickly, and firms scale up much faster than they ever did in the past. To make a clear bet on the "best fit" between seemingly conflicting cultural elements is challenging but critical. This has particular implications in cross-cultural settings, given that Chinese firms or firms doing business in China are more likely to be influenced by the Confucian "Doctrine of the Mean": that there is no clear-cut division between black and white. They intentionally prefer a gray area in the rules to allow for exceptions, and this particular preference of not making clear choices – but staying in the middle to allow for flexibility depending on the context – seems reasonable even though it's not the best way to start shaping a strong culture.

Translate Conceptual Values Into Actionable Forms of Cultural Behavior

Regardless of the type of culture that a firm makes a bet on, whether it's Silicon Valley's creative style, GM's hierarchical structure, or Huawei's military approach, their choice reflects specific beliefs, norms, and behaviors that employees are expected to follow to enhance the firm's long-term success.

Unfortunately, many firms today are committed to training about conceptual values, but not guiding actions. Both Drucker and Confucius encouraged people to practice and act on what they learned. The Confucian statement that "the Way is made in the walking of it"[82] along with Drucker's emphasis on management practices underscore the fundamental importance of value-informed actions. Obviously to shape a market requires a transformation of both mindset and behavior, but behavior is more obvious and measurable. Often employees have different understandings of how to translate the same value into different behaviors, especially when the firm operates in a cross-cultural setting. Achieving a mutual understanding between all members can be challenging, and, as a result, many firms introduce an action guide as an "official translation" of how certain values should be practiced in the firm's specific environment. This may be a sensible solution, but imposing a single unified code of conduct in today's diversified world may be met by strong internal resistance from the firm's knowledge workers.

Culture isn't static, of course; it's changeable. Cultural transformation requires taking actions to turn a desired cultural behavior into an actual habit, and this takes a long time. That is why, along with repeated educational efforts and the role model effect of the firm's executives, another solution involves creating the "right" environment with an immersion experience of the desired cultural goal. When we talk about cultural environments, we are including both physical office settings as well as the interpersonal relationships that enable employees to understand what behavior is expected in the workplace. The best example of such an immersive experience is the creation of university-like campuses in Silicon Valley. These are often designed with open spaces to encourage staff interaction and creativity, free snack and gym equipment areas, along with a higher level of tolerance, autonomy, and a flexible delayered management structure allowing for employees to work from home. Other interesting examples include Alibaba's "handstand" culture that encourages employees to think in an unexpected way, and TCT's "confession restroom" decorated with a 360-degree kaleidoscope mirror to remind employees to discover multiple truths and be mindful of multiple perspectives.

Besides their physical environment, employees base how they feel at work every day on their interactions with others. Employees at one firm might enjoy experiencing healthy competition in a "sports team" environment, while another firm encourages a culture of "constructive confrontation" and free speech or a "family culture" in which coworkers might become friends. Human interaction is especially important in firms in Confucian societies in which the traditional flourishing of culture depends on interrelationships (*guanxi*).[83]

Adhering to values-led conduct in a firm is not easy. Many firms claim that they have an innovation culture while limiting investment in R&D and research teams. The same is true of firms that say they encourage a result-driven culture but still require a clock and timekeeping system to control their employees' presence in the office. And there are still other firms that want to practice Drucker's principle of growing the skillsets of their teams, but they limit investments in training and don't prioritize team development over the financial bottom line.

That is why building a vibrant and strong culture is a time-consuming process. Helping people understand what they are expected to do is crucial; once this is accomplished, the firm can make value-informed actions that will produce real and substantial results.

Notes

1. Bernard J. Jaworski, Ajay K. Kohli, and Aryind Sahay, "Market-Driven Versus Driving Markets," *Journal of the Academy of Marketing Science* 28, 1 (2000): 45–54.
2. Bernard J. Jaworski, Ajay K. Kohli, and Shikhar Sarin, "Driving Markets: A Typology and a Seven-Step Approach," *Industrial Marketing Management* 91 (2020): 142–151.

3. Virginia Cheung, "Comparing and Contrasting the Core Philosophical Principles of Peter Drucker and Confucianism" (doctoral dissertation, Claremont Graduate University, 2020), 275.
4. Jack Beatty, *The World According to Peter Drucker* (New York: Broadway Books, 1998), 1.
5. Poola Tirupati Raju, *Introduction to Comparative Philosophy* (Lincoln, Nebraska: University of Nebraska Press, 1962), 129.
6. See note 3 above, 275.
7. "About Peter Drucker," Drucker Institute, accessed October 12, 2022, https://www.drucker.institute/perspective/about-peter-drucker/
8. Bryan Van Norden, *Introduction to Classical Chinese Philosophy* (Indianapolis: Hackett Publishing, UK edition, 2011), 99.
9. Peter Drucker, *The Essential Drucker* (New York: HarperBusiness, 2008), 313.
10. See note 5 above, 103.
11. Thomas A. Wilson, "Genealogy and History in Neo-Confucian Sectarian Uses of the Confucian Past," *Modern China* 20, no. 1 (January 1994): 3–33, doi:10.1177/009770049402000101.
12. See note 9 above, 59.
13. Peter Drucker, *The Practice of Management* (New York: Harper & Row, 1954), 37.
14. "Jack Welch's 6 Tips for Managing Employees," *Management Matters Network*, April 22, 2018, https://www.managementmattersnetwork.com/strategic-leadership/articles/jack-welchs-6-tips-for-managing-employees
15. See note 8 above, 46.
16. See note 9 above, 28.
17. Ryan Craggs, "Southwest Gets the Fewest Complaints of Any U.S. Airline," *Condé Nast Traveler*, April 7, 2017, https://www.cntraveler.com/story/southwest-gets-the-fewest-complaints-of-any-us-airline
18. "Southwest Airlines Mission Statement & Vision Statement," Mission Statements, accessed October 12, 2022, https://mission-statement.com/southwest-airlines/
19. Peter Drucker, "The Theory of the Business," *Harvard Business Review*, September-October 1994, https://hbr.org/1994/09/the-theory-of-the-business
20. Bernard J. Jaworski and Ajay K. Kohli, "Market Orientation: Construct, Research Propositions, and Managerial Implications," *Journal of Marketing* 54 (April), 1–18.
21. See note 9 above, 59.
22. See note 19 above.
23. Roger Ames and Henry Rosemont, *The Analects of Confucius: A Philosophical Translation* (New York: Ballantine, 1999), 26.
24. Confucius and Edward Slingerland, *Essential Analects* (Indianapolis: Hackett Publishing, 2006), 57; Bryan Van Norden, *Introduction to Classical Chinese Philosophy*, 19.
25. See note 8 above, 99.
26. "How Patagonia Balances Social Value and Business Value," *Socap Digital*, December 5, 2017, https://socapglobal.com/2017/12/patagonia-balances-social-value-business-value/

27. Anthony Scott, "Kodak's Downfall Wasn't About Technology," *Harvard Business Review*, July 15, 2016, https://hbr.org/2016/07/kodaks-downfall-wasnt-about-technology
28. Ibid.
29. "Mission," SpaceX, accessed October 12, 2022, https://www.spacex.com/mission/
30. "About Blue," Blue Origin, accessed October 12, 2022, https://www.blueorigin.com/about-blue/
31. See note 9 above, 61.
32. Christine Rowland, "Apple Inc.'s Mission Statement and Vision Statement (An Analysis)," Panmore Institute, May 9, 2022, https://panmore.com/apple-mission-statement-vision-statement
33. See note 23 above, 45.
34. "About Us," Traffic Control Technology, accessed October 12, 2022, https://en.bj-tct.com/about/index.html#culture
35. "Alibaba Mission and Vision Statements Analysis," Mission Statements, accessed October 12, 2022, https://mission-statement.com/alibaba/
36. Milton Friedman, "The Social Responsibility of Business Is to Increase Its Profits," in *Corporate Ethics and Corporate Governance*, eds. Zimmerli, W. C., Holzinger, M., Richter, K. Berlin, Heidelberg: Springer, 2007. doi:10.1007/978-3-540-70818-6_14
37. Goodup, accessed October 12, 2022, https://goodup.com/the-purpose-economy/
38. "Green Brands and Sustainability Branding: Definition, Concepts, Theory," accessed October 12, 2022, https://placebrandobserver.com/theory/green-brands-sustainability-branding/
39. Nikola Gemeš, "17 Green Companies That Are Good for You and The Environment," *Green Citizen*, June 5, 2022, https://greencitizen.com/blog/green-companies/
40. "Vision Statement," CFI, 2022, accessed October 12, 2022, https://corporatefinanceinstitute.com/resources/knowledge/strategy/vision-statement/
41. Chloe Berger, "Frustrated Apple Employees Reject CEO Tim Cook's Hybrid Plan by Threatening to Quit," *Fortune*, April 4, 2022, https://fortune.com/2022/04/04/apple-return-to-office-employees-threaten-quit-hybrid-work/
42. William Cohen, *Peter Drucker on Consulting* (New York: LID Publishing, 2016), 195.
43. "The Search for Purpose at Work," McKinsey, June 3, 2021, https://www.mckinsey.com/business-functions/people-and-organizational-performance/our-insights/the-search-for-purpose-at-work
44. Peter Drucker, *Post-Capitalist Society* (New York: Harper Business, 1994), 108.
45. "Case Study: Product Certification LCF-300 CBTC technology," Ricardo Rail, accessed December 8, 2022, https://rail.ricardo.com/projects/product-certification-lcf-300-cbtc-technology
46. See note 9 above, 308.
47. See note 43 above.
48. Confucius, *The Book of Rites* and *The Great Learning*, http://classics.mit.edu/Confucius/learning.html
49. "'996' Schedule Must Not Be Imposed on Workers," *Chinadaily*, April 15, 2019, https://global.chinadaily.com.cn/a/201904/15/WS5cb411e2a3104842260b63fc.html
50. See note 43 above.

51. "Tesla Mission and Vision Statement Analysis," Mission Statements, accessed October 12, 2022, https://mission-statement.com/tesla/

52. Peter Drucker, "The New Society of Organizations," *Harvard Business Review*, September-October 1992, https://hbr.org/1992/09/the-new-society-of-organizations

53. "The 10 Most Socially Responsible Companies & Brands to Model," *Grow Ensemble*, accessed October 12, 2022, https://growensemble.com/socially-responsible-companies/

54. See note 5 above, 107.

55. Henrik Bork, "How Short-Sighted Vision Turned a Chinese Success Story into a Cautionary Tale," *Roland Berger*, August 8, 2019, https://www.rolandberger.com/en/Insights/Publications/The-rise-and-fall-of-Chinese-bike-sharing-startups.html

56. Peter F. Drucker, *The Effective Executive: The Definitive Guide to Getting the Right Things Done* (New York: Collins, 2006), 55.

57. Ibid., 223.

58. Peter Drucker, *Management: Tasks, Responsibilities, Practices* (New York: Harper & Row, 1973), 29–30.

59. Also translated as "petty man" which, in contrast to a "superior person," represents the complete opposite of a virtuous person.

60. Confucius and Edward Slingerland, *Essential Analects* (Indianapolis: Hackett Publishing, 2006), 12; Analects 4.16.

61. See note 9 above, 210.

62. See note 60 above, 4; Analects 2.1.

63. See note 9 above, 223.

64. "17 Common Values," Ferguson Values, accessed October 12, 2022, https://www.fergusonvalues.com/17-common-values/

65. "Vanke, No Bribery," Schwaller et al. September 29, 2011. https://wedreambusiness.org/Vanke-No-Bribery.html

66. See note 9 above, 223.

67. Ibid.

68. "Budweiser – History, Brand Value, and Brand Strategy," *Be Next Brand*, accessed October 12, 2022, https://benextbrand.com/budweiser-history-brand-value-strategy/

69. "Wolf Spirit," Elephant Room, accessed October 12, 2022, http://elephant-room.com/2017/05/22/wolf/

70. Ibid.

71. In addition to the Five Constants, other important virtues include loyalty (*zhong*), filial piety (*xiao*), and continency (*jie*).

72. See note 60 above, 69; Analects 4.16, 14.12.

73. Peter Drucker, *A Functioning Society*, (New York: Routledge, 2003), 328.

74. "Our Values," Michelin, accessed October 12, 2022, https://www.michelin.com/en/michelin-group/purpose/values/

75. "Our Values," KraftHeinz, accessed October 12, 2022, https://www.kraftheinz.co.in/our_values

76. Melissa Bell, "Is Heinz Ketchup Harmful? Researchers Say...." *The Health Science Journal*, October 5, 2017, https://www.thehealthsciencejournal.com/heinz-ketchup-harmful-researchers-say/

77. Shel Horowitz, "Do Inventions Come from Frustration or Innovation?" *Green and Profitable*, August 21, 2010, https://greenandprofitable.com/frustration-or-innovation-blogboost/

78. Emily Fata, "5 Examples of Bureaucratic Leadership in Action," Starting Business, January 3, 2020, https://www.startingbusiness.com/blog/bureaucratic-examples

79. "Company Overview," "Great Place to Work. 2022," W. L. Gore & Associates, Inc., accessed October 12, 2022, https://www.greatplacetowork.com/certified-company/1000289

80. Steve Maich, "Spoiled, Shallow and Selfish: The New Kid at Work?" *The Canadian Encyclopedia*, December 15, 2013, https://www.thecanadianencyclopedia.ca/en/article/spoiled-shallow-and-selfish-the-new-kid-at-work

81. See note 44 above, 57.

82. See note 23 above, 33; Zhuangzi 4/2/33.

83. Ibid., 27.

Chapter 9

Drucker Management Philosophy and Ten Principles

Although management has been practiced for as long as human history, as an academic discipline it is young relative to the more traditional social and hard sciences. As Peter Drucker noted, even though it is a newer discipline, it is one of the fastest growing.[1] Drucker generally is credited with establishing the study and scope of management[2] as a separate discipline, which not only benefitted managers but also created a "management boom" in the 1950s and 1960s.[3] This increased public interest in general management theories resulted in many new people entering the field beyond traditional for-profit executives and management students.[4] Drucker crafted his management philosophy to apply to all organizations: governments, nongovernmental organizations (NGOs), nonprofits, the social sector, and traditional for-profit firms.

Peter Drucker and His Philosophy

Renowned as the "father of modern management" who "changed the face of industrial America,"[5] Drucker was also an educator, writer, journalist, and consultant. His works are widely read and respected throughout the world. One of the best-known and most influential thinkers, he wrote about management topics as well as economics, politics, and society.[6] His works have a strong social focus and are human-centered. From Drucker's perspective, management is a social discipline that enables "a functioning society." His focus on people's values, growth, and development instill his philosophy with a spirit of humanity.

Drucker worked to establish management as a separate discipline, one that could be widely studied and further developed. He asserted that management is a liberal art in practice, with transdisciplinary concepts from psychology, philosophy, history, and religion. The essence of management was "to make knowledge productive."[7] He noted: "Goals can be set. And performance can be measured.

Creating the Organization of the Future, 101–122
Emerald Publishing Limited, Howard House, Wagon Lane, Bingley BD16 1WA, UK.
First published as 当德鲁克遇见孔夫子 (*"Setting the Direction for Your Firm"*) by Orient Publishing Center ("OPC"), with Bernard Jaworski and Virginia Cheung, China, 2021. English language translation copyright © 2023, Emerald Publishing Limited. This English language edition published under exclusive licence from OPC by Emerald Publishing Limited. Translated by Bernard Jaworski and Virginia Cheung. The moral right of the copyright holder and translator has been asserted.
All rights of reproduction in any form reserved
doi:10.1108/978-1-83753-216-220231009

And then business can perform."[8] This making knowledge productive applies to how *all* organizations perform, including businesses, nonprofits, and government agencies.[9]

Ten Principles

Drucker's management philosophy contains a set of human-centered principles that can be studied from a holistic view and implemented at all levels within any organization. The Drucker School of Management at Claremont Graduate University and the Drucker Institute crafted these principles from the entirety of Drucker's writings. Jaworski took those principles and created "behavior anchors" to score each principle. The anchors translate each general principle into specific criteria that make it easy for executives to score their organizations on the principles. While they cover a broad array of Drucker's thinking, these principles do not substitute for an in-depth, comprehensive study of his philosophy.

Clear Mission and Theory of the Business

Every organization needs a purpose and a mission statement (see Fig. 9.1). A clear mission statement articulates the organization's reason for being. A clear mission statement also answers the fundamental question, "What business are we in?" Drucker stated that having this "enables a business to set objectives, to develop strategies, to concentrate its resources, and to go to work. It alone enables a business to be managed for performance."[10] A mission sets a common goal for all and enables everyone to align their roles to the mission. It provides guidance for decision-making as well as a framework for what to do and what *not* to do. When properly crafted, it enables the organization to stay focused - and sets boundaries regarding which businesses to be in and which ones it should not be in.

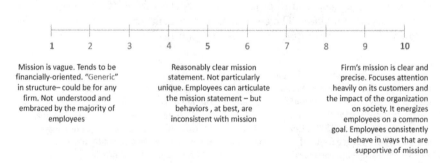

Fig. 9.1.   Clear Mission and Theory of the Business.

A mission statement articulates what makes a business different from all others. To be effective, it must be customer-based, focused on a clear segment (or segments) and identifies the underlying need of each particular customer group. This process may involve trade-offs as the values of any given customer group may not be the same as what other groups have. Take the example of the fashion industry. For luxury brands, the most sought after customer value is the prestigious status their customers perceive because of the limited supply of certain designs, high prices, and the quality of customized services. For fast fashion brands, though, target customers value the latest trends but at a reasonable price even if it means lower quality. Both types of brands provide customer value, but their distinct values attract different customer groups. So, organizations need to make a clear choice about which customer groups they are going to serve according to their resources and competence.

Drucker suggests that organizations should examine (or reexamine) their business definition when the business is successful, rather than in decline.[11] He cautions that it's not always an easy exercise and the answers may not be obvious.[12]

Defining "what business we are in" requires systematic analysis to develop a deep understanding of an organization's internal operations and resources, including existing products and services, resource distribution, daily operations, and the external environment, such as societal change, industry change, and changes in customers, markets, and values. A well-defined mission aligns the organization's internal core competence with its external environment and reflects the core characteristics of the market as well as the features that make it different from others. As Drucker noted, it must fit the assumptions of the external marketplace.

Further, a focused mission defines not only what a business should and shouldn't do but also aligns managers with what business their company should be in. Considering today's fast-changing business environment, managers must successfully navigate to be effective. As Drucker noted many times, the root cause of crisis is not doing the wrong things, but doing the right things that don't fit the present reality.[13] Therefore, organizations need to regularly ask the question that Drucker asked Welch – the former CEO of General Electric to not only define the present, but also to prepare for a transition into the future. Managers must be aware that whenever the macro environment changes in fundamental ways, the organization must reconsider its mission and "what it gets paid for." This is what Drucker called the "theory of the business," and he believed every organization needs one.[14]

The question "what business are we in?" involves the balance between short-term and long-term organizational goals, while the question "what business should we be in?" involves the analysis of what is right and whether the organization's existing business needs to be changed.[15] "What is right" can be complex, and many considerations must be taken into account with customer value and social impact being two significant determining factors. As mentioned earlier, the inclusion of customer value in the mission statement can provide key stakeholders with a deeper understanding of the business. Take the example of popular yoga gear producer lululemon, whose mission is "to elevate the world by unleashing the full potential within every one of us." This statement indicates the company is not limited to providing the physical product of yoga gear but also offers customers a deeper value: the health and freedom to unleash their full potential in life.

To effectively "manage by objectives," managers and employees must translate the organization's mission into multiple operational objectives. If an organization needs to redefine its mission to switch to new business, its objectives must change accordingly. In turn, these new objectives will require a series of internal changes from structural to operational resources.

Commitment to a mission requires effective implementation. This means that everyone within the organization—at all levels—must understand the mission and be able align their activities and results with the mission. A mission must be clear and focused. As Drucker noted, it should "fit on a T-shirt."

Focus on Understanding Customer Needs

One of Drucker's most widely recognized quotes is, "The only valid definition of business purpose is to create a customer."[16] A market is formed by customer demand and is fundamentally driven by the customer. As Drucker noted, "It is the customer who determines what a business is."[17] Therefore, because an organization needs to focus on customers, the manager's most important task is to define its customers, identify needs, and fulfill them. It is a process of customer value creation. What customers need is not just a physical product and services, but the value derived from products and services they buy (see Fig. 9.2).

Drucker also introduced the concept of unarticulated demand from the customer, which he termed as "unfelt want"—that is, a need customers do not know until they see it. The best contemporary example would be the smartphone. When the market was still dominated by Nokia cellular phones, customers could not imagine how a disruptive innovation like the smartphone could change their

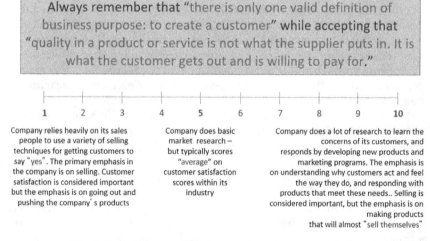

Fig. 9.2.   Focus on Understanding Customer Needs.

lifestyle. Visionary organizations that can continually recognize unfelt needs and wants will survive and prosper in the market. Apple was able to "see" customer unfelt needs far ahead of the customers themselves.

Drucker's concept of "creating customers" provides organizations with an even higher requirement beyond knowing the customer well enough to identify their existing needs. Creating new value, new demand, and new customers is the constant challenge for a business. This leads to two entrepreneurial functions of business: marketing and innovation.[18] Using marketing to understand the voice of customer and then innovating new products and services to create new value drives the economic performance of an organization.

That said, being able to identify new customers and new value is not the end result by which to measure managers' effectiveness—rather, it is the ability to translate potential market demand into business opportunities that generate positive economic returns. Organizations have the responsibility to allocate their resources effectively to supply quality products and services at costs that match demand. This wealth and value-producing process is a manager's most important job.[19] As Drucker said, "The customer is the foundation of a business and keeps it in existence. He alone gives employment. And it is to supply the consumer that society entrusts wealth-producing resources to the business enterprise."[20]

Responsibility and Accountability at All Levels

Since Drucker developed the concept of the knowledge worker, it has become a widely used and accepted concept. In this new knowledge economy, the traditional "command and control" managerial mode from the early days of industrialization is no longer applicable. Today we see much less of the "boss and subordinate" relationship between executives and employees, whom Drucker termed "associates" rather than "subordinates" without clear rank.[21] In modern organizations, not all decisions have to come from top executives. Everyone in knowledge organizations "must think through their objectives and their contributions, and take responsibility for both ... regardless of his or her particular job."[22] Drucker asserted decentralization as a must, saying that each and every knowledge worker in modern organizations is their own "executive."[23] Any employee who can be held accountable for using his or her knowledge to make responsible decisions and to contribute to the overall performance and results can be regarded as his or her own "executive."[24]

This principle is visionary considering that in Drucker's time a few industry giants dominated the marketplace. Those large organizations exercised centralized management. However, as modern organizations started to evolve, top executives become more dependent on mid-level managers and executives in sub-business units to perform for themselves. If the organization wants to maintain its innovative spirit, it needs to intentionally drive responsibility and accountability deep into the organization (see Fig. 9.3). Equally, these mid-level managers need to grow their lower-ranked front-line employees, allowing them to make their independent decisions to deliver performance. As Drucker commented on General Motors, "Their operating managers have to have the freedom to do things their own way. They have to have responsibility and the authority that goes with it. They have to have scope to show what they can do, and they have to get recognition for performance ... (this is) even more important as a company gets older and as it has to depend on developing strong, independent performing executives from within."[25] Drucker's intention in promoting knowledge workers is not to make everyone a boss but to make everyone a contributor.[26]

This principle fits today's delayered horizontal organizations perfectly. Here everyone is expected to be an autonomous part of the decision-making process,[27] so they can quickly react to a constantly changing environment. This phenomenon is particularly obvious when we see an organization with diversified products. The business is normally split into several subunits based on products and decentralized within each of these subunits to allow them to grow in their own markets. The popularity of delayering demonstrates the visionary nature of this principle.

Although Drucker encouraged autonomy, decentralization does not mean each individual can determine his or her own work. On the contrary, Drucker heavily focused on alignment between individual goals, team goals, and organizational goals through the framework of management by objectives. Employees are truly accountable and responsible when they are not solely thinking from their own role but instead focused on how their contributions can better serve the overall purpose of the organization. Knowledge workers normally bring their own specialized knowledge. In contrast to the traditional "command and control" mode in which executives set goals for everyone, effective knowledge workers are able to draw out individual objectives that best utilize their specialized knowledge to align with organizational needs. Letting everyone be their own executives actually places more responsibility on both knowledge workers and executives. As such it places more demands on the worker and the enterprise. Yet, for

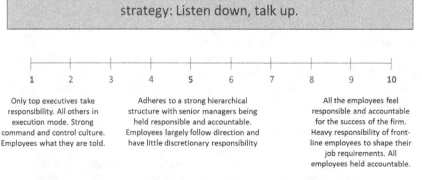

Push responsibility and accountability as far down into the organization as possible and follow this basic communications strategy: Listen down, talk up.

1	2	3	4	5	6	7	8	9	10

Only top executives take responsibility. All others in execution mode. Strong command and control culture. Employees what they are told.

Adheres to a strong hierarchical structure with senior managers being held responsible and accountable. Employees largely follow direction and have little discretionary responsibility

All the employees feel responsible and accountable for the success of the firm. Heavy responsibility of front-line employees to shape their job requirements. All employees held accountable.

Fig. 9.3.   Responsibility and Accountability at All Levels.

organizations that are willing to build up their long-term comparative advantage based on people, this principle allows them to better leverage knowledge workers' unleashed full potential.

In this fast-changing market, it is often the case that front-line employees know their customer the best. Considering that they are knowledge workers, it is simply more effective to let them make decisions based on their best knowledge. Knowledge workers are not to be supervised in every detail; they should be able to manage themselves effectively to deliver results.[28] As Drucker explained, "Organizations must be able to make fast decisions, based on closeness to performance, closeness to market, closeness to technology, closeness to the changes in society, environment, and demographics."[29] Overall organizational performance is a joint force that cannot be accomplished by anyone alone; it requires everyone to be accountable and responsible for their own tasks. Therefore, decision-making cannot just come from the top down. As Drucker often pointed out, "Low-level decisions are extremely important in a knowledge-based organization."[30]

Pushing accountability down, from Drucker's point of view, encourages people to concentrate on their strengths and their most important tasks, and to delegate issues for which they do not have specialized knowledge.[31] So executives should encourage front-line employees to drive resolution and shape a dynamic and changing organizational culture with higher staff engagement. This can result in greater customer satisfaction and improved financial performance. It is the managers' job to make sure "the responsible people in their organizations perform."[32] Giving knowledge workers' responsibility gives them ownership over their work, they can better align their vision and their work with overall organizational needs and make a greater impact.

Some Drucker scholars think decentralization works only when everyone in the organization is a knowledge worker who is sufficiently competent to make "smart decisions," and this may not be possible in reality.[33] But Drucker had deep faith in the idea that every executive would rather be motivated to "step up" and take the lead on objectives and be held accountable. The essence of this principle—to push accountability and responsibility down—is to give every employee the chance to take the lead and grow.

Employee Orientation

The principle that "employees are not costs to cut, they are resources to preserve"[34] best reflects the fundamental human spirit of Drucker's philosophy. Drucker defines an organization as "the place to convert knowledge workers' specialized knowledge into performance, to make them effective."[35] This definition gives an organization the function and responsibility to develop people, train them in their roles, and grow them to be effective (see Fig. 9.4).

As Drucker put it, "A manager develops people."[36] One of a manager's most important jobs is to develop his or her team, and this is often a performance measure by which a team leader's effectiveness is measured. "To make the worker achieving is, therefore, more and more important and is a measure of the performance of an institution,"[37] Drucker said. Organizations should be willing to invest in people's

1	2	3	4	5	6	7	8	9	10

Places very little emphasis on the development of employees. Low level of employee loyalty. Frequently experiences high employee turnover.	Engages in employee development through training programs but only at a very basic level. Employee satisfaction and loyalty scores are in the "middle of the pack" in their industry	Develops programs around professional and personal development of its employees. Viewed as world class in talent development. Deeply loyal employees. Employees are aggressively targeted by competitors or others outside the industry

Fig. 9.4.   Employee Orientation.

development, whether it is professional or personal. Organizations, for example, could provide training to enhance employees' specialized knowledge, such as continuous study on technical advancement, developing soft skills in communication and leadership, or taking care of employees' physical and mental health.

Further, as interrelated with the previous principle, Drucker distinctly suggested development through contribution. That is, executives can grow employees by delegation—by providing people with more opportunities to try challenging tasks and setting a higher standard of merits to shape a culture of excellence. Encouraging contribution gives people room to develop their effectiveness, achieve material gains through monetary payments and social status, and achieve emotional gains through self-realization and satisfaction in this process.[38] As Drucker said, "Focus on contribution by itself is a powerful force in developing people."[39]

Drucker also pointed out that growth can come from developing others and from self-development.[40] In addition to the responsibility to develop others, he provided a set of methods to develop oneself through self-management. Individuals can and should always develop themselves through better self-management skills while also developing others.

As Drucker said, "One does not 'manage' people. The task is to lead people. And the goal is to make productive the specific strengths and knowledge of each individual."[41] Making a knowledge worker productive requires a management-by-objectives framework to identify personal value, strength, and responsibility; align personal goals with a common goal; and promote teamwork.[42] This human-centered principle requires managers to consider the issue of putting people in the right roles that fit their values to unleash their full potential because Drucker argued that "performance is built on strength not on weakness."[43]

It takes time, effort, and resources to nurture employees for significant improvements in performance. This may raise a concern about the "return on investment" with people, and there is also the risk that employees may leave for other jobs once they've realized their professional potential. That is why many organizations prefer to hire "established employees" with skillsets that can be readily used rather than training existing employees in these skills. In Drucker's view, though, people are an organization's most important resources, and it benefits the organization when employees "acquire the capacity to grow, to develop, to contribute through management."[44] In fact, organizations that invest in their employees have greater workforce loyalty and higher retention rates.[45] Higher employee satisfaction can lead to higher customer satisfaction[46] because every employee is focused on making a contribution.

Drucker's human-centered management focus transformed the traditional managerial mindset. The "employ the whole person" concept implies that organizations need to accept each employee as multidimensional with "good" and "bad" qualities. Therefore, organizations should give everyone an equal chance and resources to help them grow. Effective managers should assign knowledge workers to the roles that best fit them and treat everyone equally regardless of their particular positions.

Everyone Innovates

Long before there were comprehensive studies on innovation and entrepreneurship, Drucker wrote this about the importance of innovation: "Not to innovate is the single largest reason for the decline of existing organizations."[47]

Conventional wisdom has it that technological advancement drives human and economic development, but Drucker defined innovation as any "effect in economy and society."[48] In other words, any action that creates a new dimension of performance can be an innovation. Drucker emphasized that this broader range of social, systemic, and process innovations is just as important in our lives as natural science or technological invention (see Fig. 9.5).

Innovation improves productivity and can itself be a measure of productivity. As Drucker asserted, productivity and performance are built on specific strengths and knowledge.[49] For Drucker, innovation too is based on one's strengths. Successful innovation should start from small, tentative, and flexible experiments.[50] As Drucker said, "Innovation, by definition, has to be decentralized, ad hoc, autonomous, specific, and microeconomic."[51] Innovation is not limited to the R&D department or to a small group of executives; it is the responsibility of everyone, at all levels of the organization. Everyone should have a point of view from their role and an opinion on how to achieve common goals innovatively as a team. Therefore, all knowledge workers within the organization, who know their respective functions best, can and should innovate in their roles to create a positive impact on the overall performance. This is because innovation mostly "happens close to events."[52]

As Drucker asserted, innovation should be market-driven and evidence-based. Obtaining a holistic view to capture all evidence in a changing market environment requires effort from everyone, at all levels, for innovation to be effective. If,

Fig. 9.5.   Everyone Innovates.

for example, the organization aims to incubate innovation in customer experience, it must consider a broad range of information from all functions with touchpoints to customers, together with the engagement of R&D, for the best solution. Front-line employees, in particular, are closest to the market and customers—they know best what the problems are and what improvements are needed to optimize their operation and customer handling. These front-line employees should be accountable and responsible for making decisions in response to market changes. For the same reason, organizations should encourage these front-line employees to drive the resolution for improvement. This is what Drucker called "knowledge-based innovation." As Drucker said himself, "Innovation has to be close to the market, focused on the market, it is indeed market-driven."[53]

There are varying methods to incubate an innovative culture within the organization, including brainstorming without judgment, collaboration, teamwork, and information-sharing across functions. Innovation may involve fast-paced prototyping along with the appropriate risk-taking. Resilience against inevitable failures is essential in this process.

To be sure, any innovation involves risk-taking, Drucker addressed this, explaining that innovation "is risky . . . all economic activity is by definition 'high risk.' And defending yesterday—that is, not innovating—is far more risky than making tomorrow."[54] Therefore, the key to letting everyone innovate is encouraging everyone to look for innovative opportunities in their daily obstacles and customer pain points. These innovations can be just small process changes with definable risk to position the organization as "opportunity focused" rather than "risk focused."[55] Innovation can also be tentative if it doesn't reach the expected and desired result; with small start-up cost and resources, innovation-associated risks can be minimized.[56] If an organization can follow this principle to start its innovation journey—encouraging small changes at all levels, capturing potentially innovative opportunities—these small innovations can have a big impact on the organization in the long term and shape a culture of innovation and excellence. Because innovation can exist in many places within an organization's daily operations, it may not come as planned, but if the organization can stay opportunity-focused, innovation can happen and be managed.

Regular Abandonment Is Practiced

"What exists is getting old."[57] It is our natural human tendency to cling to "yesterday's successes."[58] This phenomenon applies to well-established organizations with long histories and strong cultures, and, on the individual level, to successful executives with a long track record of success. In this knowledge era, when knowledge changes quickly, the experiences, skills, and processes that we are comfortable with and have proved to work will limit our growth if we don't practice systematic abandonment.[59] Especially when these "successful experiences" have deeply rooted norms and beliefs about how things are supposed to work, often successful firms may stop asking whether what worked yesterday still works for tomorrow and assume they have the right business model. Many do not realize that those old ways of working may be obsolete or no longer applicable in today's environment. Abandonment is, therefore, a process to make space to create the new for tomorrow, to clear the path for continuous success in the future (see Fig. 9.6).

This abandonment process is not a one-time task. Rather, it needs to be practiced on a regular basis. As Drucker asserted, regular abandonment needs to be a planned event in organizations, and "past decisions, policies, strategies need to be revisited, challenged, made to justify themselves in terms of the challenge of

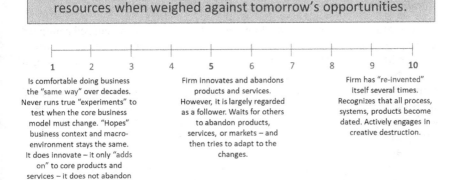

Fig. 9.6. Regular Abandonment Is Practiced.

the new."[60] What to abandon can also be a test of the organization's vision; it's an issue of what it imagines tomorrow will look like.

Visionary executives come with experience and knowledge of how something worked in the past, as well as a clear vision of the desired results in the future. Based on this knowledge, effective executives can make their abandonment plan to prepare for the future by asking themselves the question, "If we were going to start our business all over again today, knowing what we now know, what would we do?"[61]

Regular abandonment is necessary because where we are today is based on yesterday's decisions and actions. With limited time and energy, effective executives do "first things first," prioritizing the important issues for tomorrow so that they cannot live on yesterday's success or problems. Necessary abandonment of what is no longer applicable helps an organization focus on what works today and what works for tomorrow. Only then can the organization build the competence needed for tomorrow.

In this way, regular abandonment can be practiced as a tool to achieve effectiveness and productivity in organizational life. Abandonment is necessary to clear the road for innovation. As Drucker wrote, "The first rule for the concentration of executive efforts is to slough off the past that has ceased to be productive."[62] That suggests that executives must regularly review their own work as well as their subordinates' work, make the right choice to drop activities that are no longer productive, and to concentrate on essential issues that can produce results and performance so that organizations can be more effective and produce innovations that result in a bigger impact.

It is, however, not an easy task. It takes effort and certain risk-taking to implement regular abandonment; as mentioned previously, there is often strong resistance within the organization to discard norms, especially those that have been effective in the past. Drucker explained that such resistance always favors "what has happened over the future, the crisis over the opportunity, the immediate and visible over the real, and the urgent over the relevant."[63]

Results, Not Activities, Are Measured for All Stakeholders

Contrary to the conventional wisdom that often focuses on an itemized action list, Drucker asserted that actions should produce results. Thus, to be results-driven, we should concentrate on activities that can produce results. "All one can measure," he wrote, "and should measure is performance."[64] One key feature of Drucker's management philosophy is being "results-oriented, outcome-based, peer-focused, and performance-driven."[65] Drucker created a set of criteria to evaluate organizational and individual performance. This principle adds significant practical meaning to his philosophy (see Fig. 9.7).

On an individual level, Drucker suggested that "effective executives focus on results, not on work."[66] It is the tendency for not just executives but every individual in the organization to count on their efforts and specific tasks accomplished rather than the result produced by these tasks. Being responsible for the result is

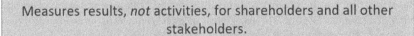

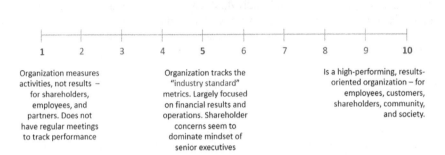

Fig. 9.7.   Results, Not Activities, Are Measured for All Stakeholders.

the key to effectiveness since not every task can produce the desired results, and not all tasks produce an equal rate of return. To best allocate resources to the most productive tasks, then, an organization should take results rather than the work itself as a measure of performance. In fact, Drucker defines an organization as a special purpose institution to produce results.[67] By this definition, an organization is not performing its function and is wasting scarce resources if it works on tasks that cannot deliver results. "One should hold oneself accountable for the performance of the whole,"[68] he wrote, suggesting that employees should always check whether they are making the contribution required for the overall organizational need.

Although Drucker required results to be clear, unambiguous, and measurable,[69] measuring results can be a complex task. Doing so requires a holistic, 360-degree view from different stakeholders. Countless internal and external factors can affect the final result of a particular task, and certain jobs are just harder to measure. These determining factors also can include local societal culture, organizational culture, industry features and norms, as well as the specific function, the role of the person being evaluated, and so on. Different voices, such as employees, customers, shareholders, and the general public, should be heard and taken into account. All these factors affect the effectiveness of a performance evaluation.

Measurement of performance has no fixed rules, but doing it correctly requires effective communications to align the expectations between employees and executives. Employees should have a full understanding of what is expected of them and how they are going to be measured and judged.

Consider Drucker's three main yardsticks of performance: direct results, building values and their reaffirmation, and building and developing people for tomorrow.[70] Organizations need direct economic results to maintain their operations and sustainability, so profitability is always a primary measurement. But while profit is important, Drucker also suggests that executives must employ other measurements and not use financial performance as the only criterion. There are other outputs that can contribute to a positive social impact, such as the professional development of employees, building values, and so on. Effective organizations, executives, and individual employees should all focus on the activities that can produce the most direct output when they allocate their resources with consideration toward measuring all outcomes, not just financial outputs.

Balances Short-Term and Long-Term Results

"Effective managers should be able to manage both present and future."[71] As the previous principle suggests, multiple perspectives are needed to measure results and evaluate performance. The choice of how to allocate resources involves a trade-off. Effective executives should have a good understanding of the current situation and problems, but they should also have a clear vision of the future. They must balance resource allocation for the organization to stay effective and productive from year to year yet at the same time build competence for sustainability so that the organization can smoothly transition from the present to the future (see Fig. 9.8).

The primary precondition for both current operation and sustainability is profitability. All other yardsticks of performance, such as building value and growing people, depend on financial support from profitability. As Drucker said, "It is the management responsibility for for-profit business enterprises to produce at least minimum profitability required to hedge future risk and uncertainties."[72] This statement demonstrates the fundamental importance of profit-making to keep the organization competitive in both the short term and the long term, so

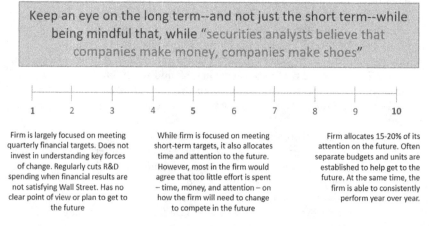

Fig. 9.8.   Balances Short Term and Long-Term Results.

profitability should be always the primary consideration for organizations to plan their path and resources. An organization is an organ of society that helps that society to function—thus, it is not a contradiction for that organization to make a profit and also exercise social responsibility. However, as Drucker noted, it is only possible to exercise social responsibility when making a profit.

To be profitable in both the short term and the long term, organizations must regularly revisit the sustainability of their current business. As suggested in previous principles, an organization's business today may not be the same business it should be tomorrow. To effectively manage from past to future between different businesses, managers need to embrace the concept of "ambidextrous organization."[73] This means to not only "look backward constantly to attend to the products and processes of the past," but also to stay forward-thinking to "prepare for the innovations that will define the future." In this case, Drucker's management-by-objectives framework requires a series of internal changes that will dictate the reallocation of resources. In this process, it is normal for organizations to have different priorities in the short term and the long term; the transition to future long-term gains may likely require a tradeoff of short-term loss. This short-term loss applies to the overall organization, but it's more likely to have an unequal share of loss within the organization—some departments and function groups may suffer more than others. Understandably, this may cause strong internal resistance to change, which is why executives need to redesign short-term objectives and measurements for performance to encourage the desired long-term change and to use effective communications so that everyone is aligned.

In addition to the concern of short-term financial loss, making a strategic choice that will benefit a business in the long term can be difficult from a value-fit perspective. An organization that is not value-fit may have good monetary return in the short term, so in this case it may need to consider and balance the tradeoff between short-term financial gain and long-term value for branding recognition and sustainability. A truly value-fit strategy should be able to balance both short-term and long-term goals that resonate with the customer groups the organization serves. In fact, financial interest, values, and social contributions may not necessarily be contractionary choices—smart organizations should be able to harmonize these different needs around their long-term goals to decide which business opportunities to pursue. Value fit is another compelling Drucker principle that is interrelated in deciding how to balance short-term and long-term results.

To be effective in resource allocation for the future without too much expense on today's operation, executives should allocate 20% of their time and resources to prepare for tomorrow's business until that future business grows solid—at which point they can start to allocate more resources into the new unit until it's time to make a complete shift. It is crucial for executives to have the vision to balance continuity and change and distribute the best portion of their time and resources to invest in the future, rather than concentrate solely on current economic performance and risk being left behind by a changing market.

Everyone Lives by the Same Values

As Drucker noted, "Every organization needs a commitment to values and constant reaffirmation, just as the human body needs vitamins and minerals. They are what 'this organization stands for.'"[74] The first Drucker principle emphasizes the importance of a well-defined mission statement and values; this principle is focused on living those values. This means that once the organizational values are identified, they must be fully understood by everyone at all levels across the organization. For that to happen, these conceptual values must be translated into practical behaviors and implemented in every aspect in an organization's operation so that these values guide business conduct. For the values to be well understood by all, they must be clear and explicit (see Fig. 9.9). As Drucker wrote, "Value commitments, like results, are not unambiguous."[75]

For Drucker, organizational values should be a unified code of conduct that applies to all business units and is applicable to the overall society; that said, there shouldn't be a separate value and ethics system for the organization and another for individuals, families, and schools.[76] So, living with values is not only important on an organizational level, they are also central to maintaining the overall function of society. Just as Drucker explained, "In a moral society, the public good must always rest on private virtue."[77]

What's more, Drucker explained that "Organizations have to have values,"[78] and building values is one major measurement of organizational performance.[79] Although values of different organizations may vary, once values are stated, everyone within the organization must buy into them. Without a strong commitment to shared values, there is no enterprise.[80] These shared organizational values are the fundamental basis for shaping the culture regarding "how it works here." That being said, these shared values should become a common belief

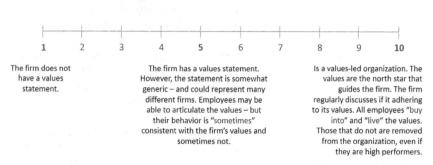

Fig. 9.9.   Everyone Lives by the Values.

for all. Value-led behaviors should become the norm to direct people's daily behavior.

This suggests why value fit is a must for individuals to live with unified organizational values. Even in the case of high-performing employees, if they do not agree with the shared values, they should be removed. Organizations need to be value-led in addition to performance-led. This is because values are "the ultimate test" according to Drucker. If an employee's strengths do not fit their value systems, even if they can perform well in their task, this job may still not be the one "to devote his life in."[81] Drucker explained this with his personal experience, that although he had the strength to be a high performer in a bank, it was not the perfect value fit job for him.[82] Therefore, Drucker suggests although one's personal values may not be exactly the same as an organization's values, they should be at least "compatible for one to be effective to produce results."[83] Value fit is the precondition for employees to live with the values, so organizations should ensure that their values are clearly articulated and effectively communicated to all. Employees must be able to state the values to understand how these values can guide their work.

However, organizations should also consider the fact that different stakeholders may perceive values differently. It is very understandable that customers may have different values from shareholders and other stakeholders. This is why, for values to be effectively implemented in a value-led organization, the organization must be in the value-fit business and adhere to value-fit business conduct.

To be in the value-fit business, Drucker asserts that once an organization has clearly defined its organizational values, it should "refrain from tackling tasks that do not fit into its value system ... as a result, it will do damage rather than good."[84] Although different organizations may have a varying focus on their values, Drucker encourages organizations to "do the right thing" to engage in ethical business. It is, however, the managers' responsibility to set the right objective to lead the organization into the right business for them, as Drucker explained: "Managers have to base their decisions on what is right rather than on what is acceptable."[85]

To adhere to value-led conduct requires a group of like-minded employees who are engaged and passionate about company values, with a sense of purpose and the ability to see the value of their work in relation to the overall organization. This will enable them to take responsibility for their actions and fully integrate organizational values into every aspect of their daily work, rather than paying lip service to them.

Demonstrate Social Responsibility

As one of the important thinkers on social problems, Drucker viewed social responsibility as an essential value for all workers. A functioning society is one of Drucker's main aims in his overall body of work. Creating a functioning society requires effective management, whether the organization is a for-profit business, a government agency, or a nonprofit. As he said, "Management worldwide has become the new social function."[86] It was for the purpose of solving social problems that Drucker introduced many of his innovative management terms, such as management by objectives and decentralization (see Fig. 9.10).

Social responsibility to Drucker was a management responsibility rather than business responsibility.[87] With the increasing attention on social responsibility, Drucker recognized "The new demand is for business to make social values and beliefs, create freedom for the individual, and produce the good society."[88] Some social problems are byproducts of an organization's operation; an organization can have a positive or negative impact on society. Other problems that exist in society due to the "sickness of government"[89] are problems that arise from society itself. Organizations can do for society what is needed when the government fails. But Drucker advocated that organizations have social functions regardless of the cause of the problem, "even though the cause of society's sickness is none of management's making."[90] Both "social impacts and social responsibility have to be managed,"[91] and as an organ in society, organizations carry this "specific social means and purpose."[92] There's a reciprocal relationship between organizations and society: If society is "unhealthy" and not functioning, organizations could be affected, too. A better society, as the prerequisite for a healthy and growing organization, is in management's self-interest too.[93] Since every employee shares some duties in the overall organizational goal, this organizational duty to social problems becomes the common goal to engage both executives and employees until the practice of social responsibility becomes the norm and organizational value for everyone to live with. Drucker described the mutual need between organizations and society as "the responsibilities of one to another, the tension that arises from the organization's need for autonomy and society's stake in the common good, the rising demand for socially responsible organizations."[94]

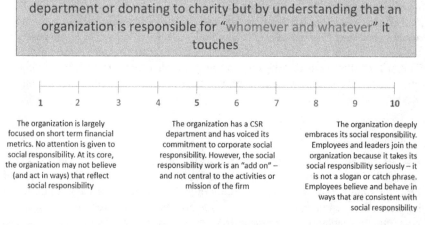

Fig. 9.10.   Demonstrates Social Responsibility.

Social responsibility as a management responsibility lies at all levels within the organization; it's not just the task of a single department nor does it rest fully on the shoulders of a small group of executives. Organizations have the full responsibility for social impact due to their own operation,[95] and it is management's job to identify and anticipate these impacts effectively. These impacts can be complex, with intended and unintended, desirable and undesirable, anticipated and unanticipated consequences. Once the impacts are identified, resolution-driven activities should be planned according to measurable results on the outputs produced from certain activities, outcomes, and impacts. To implement these planned activities, everyone in the organization must be committed to social responsibility in their own roles. It is a collective responsibility and an ongoing process. For social responsibility to grow at all levels, the organization must have a team of like-minded individuals who believe in this purpose and are willing to behave in ways that are consistent with social responsibility.

This principle would be challenging if the organization was solely aimed for profit maximization and ignored its social function. Although being profitable is an organization's first responsibility[96] and necessary to provide financial support to socially responsible activities, profit-making does not have to be in contradiction with social responsibility. Being socially responsible is not limited to philanthropy by volunteering time or donating money. On the contrary, Drucker suggested that if visionary managers could solve certain social problems effectively and innovatively, there was a chance to turn social problems into profitable business opportunities. This is, however, a higher level of requirement for organizations, one that requires innovation and vision. In addition to developing new business opportunities, there are numerous economic benefits to making an existing business socially responsible, such as positive brand recognition and public relations, greater customer loyalty, and better retention of market share.

There are, however, also certain limitations organizations should be aware of when they exercise their functions and responsibilities to solve social problems. Organizations must be focused to be effective.[97] If the organization engages in a task that is not a value fit or beyond its legitimate power or competence of knowledge and resources, it could endanger the performance of its own operation—that would be socially irresponsible.[98] All of Drucker's principles, such as being results-driven, measuring performance, promoting innovation, focusing on the task that fits one's strengths and articulating organizational values—should be the guiding principles for an organization's social responsibility.

Notes

1. Peter Drucker, *The Essential Drucker: Selections from the Management Works of Peter F. Drucker* (New York: Harper Business, 2001), 312.
2. "About Peter Drucker," Drucker Institute, accessed October 12, 2022, https://www.drucker.institute/perspective/about-peter-drucker/; Jack Beatty, *The World According to Drucker: The Life and Work of the World's Greatest Management Thinker* (London: Orion Business, 1998), 104; Peter F. Drucker, *The Practice of Management* (New York: Harper Business, 1993), viii.

3. Jack Beatty, *The World According to Peter Drucker* (New York: Broadway Books, 1998), 101.
4. See note 1 above, viii.
5. See note 3 above, 1.
6. "About Peter Drucker," Drucker Institute, accessed October 12, 2022, https://www.drucker.institute/perspective/about-peter-drucker/
7. See note 1 above, 313.
8. Ibid., 61.
9. Ibid., 72.
10. Ibid., 28.
11. Ibid., 27.
12. Peter Drucker, *The Practice of Management* (New York: Harper & Row, 1954), 49.
13. Peter F. Drucker, "The Theory of the Business," *Harvard Business Review*, September/October 1994, https://hbr.org/1994/09/the-theory-of-the-business
14. Ibid.
15. See note 12 above, 57.
16. Ibid., 37.
17. Ibid.
18. Ibid., 39.
19. Ibid., 41.
20. Ibid., 37.
21. Peter F. Drucker, *Post-Capitalist Society* (New York: Harper Business, 1994), 56.
22. Ibid., 108.
23. Ibid., 60.
24. See note 1 above, 194.
25. Peter F. Drucker, *The Effective Executive: The Definitive Guide to Getting the Right Things Done* (New York: Collins, 2006), 120.
26. See note 21 above, 109.
27. See note 1 above, 260.
28. See note 25 above, 4.
29. See note 21 above, 60.
30. See note 25 above, xvii.
31. Ibid., xiii.
32. See note 1 above, 128.
33. See note 3 above, 119.
34. Ibid., 171.
35. See note 1 above, 308.
36. See note 12 above, 298; See note 3 above, 110.
37. Peter F. Drucker, *Management: Tasks, Responsibilities, Practices* (New York: Harper & Row, 1973), 41.
38. See note 1 above, 216.
39. Ibid., 211.
40. See note 12 above, 187.
41. See note 1 above, 81.
42. Ibid., 125.
43. See note 25 above, 77–81.
44. See note 37 above, 29.

45. Bryan Adkins and David Caldwell, "Firm or Subgroup Culture: Where Does Fitting in Matter Most?" *Journal of Organizational Behavior* 25, no. 8 (December 2004), 969–978. doi:10.1002/job.291.
46. Lale Gumusluoglu and Arzu Ilsev, "Transformational Leadership, Creativity, and Organizational Innovation," *Journal of Business Research* 62, no. 4 (April 2009), 461–473, doi:10.1016/j.jbusres.2007.07.032.
47. See note 1 above, 8.
48. Ibid., 278.
49. Ibid., 81.
50. Ibid., 274–277.
51. Peter F. Drucker, *Innovation and Entrepreneurship: Practice and Principles* (New York: Harper Business, 1993), 135.
52. See note 1 above, 324.
53. Ibid., 278.
54. See note 51 above, 139; See note 3 above, 165.
55. See note 1 above, 322.
56. Ibid., 322.
57. See note 3 above, 123.
58. See note 37 above, 84–85.
59. See note 21 above, 57.
60. See note 3 above, 123.
61. Ibid., 125.
62. See note 25 above, 104.
63. Ibid., 115; See note 3 above, 126.
64. Ibid., 86.
65. Ibid., 28.
66. See note 3 above, 125.
67. See note 21 above, 53–54.
68. See note 25 above, 53.
69. See note 21 above, 55.
70. See note 25 above, 55.
71. Ibid., 59.
72. Ibid., 59.
73. Charles A. O'Reilly III and Michael L. Tushman, "The Ambidextrous Organization," *Harvard Business Review*, April 2004, https://hbr.org/2004/04/the-ambidextrous-organization
74. See note 1 above, 210.
75. Ibid., 210.
76. Ibid., 64.
77. See note 12 above, 339.
78. See note 1 above, 223.
79. Ibid., 209.
80. See note 37 above, 229–230.
81. See note 1 above, 223.
82. Ibid., 223.
83. Ibid., 223.
84. Ibid., 60.
85. Peter F. Drucker, *A Functioning Society* (New York: Routledge, 2003), 328.

86. See note 1 above, 8.
87. Ibid., 55.
88. See note 37 above, 319.
89. See note 1 above, 51.
90. Ibid., 52.
91. See note 37 above, 325.
92. See note 1 above, 14; See note 37 above, 30.
93. Ibid., 52.
94. Peter F. Drucker, "The New Society of Organizations," *Harvard Business Review*, September–October 1992, https://hbr.org/1992/09/the-new-society-of-organizations
95. See note 21 above, 102.
96. See note 21 above, 101.
97. Ibid., 43.
98. See note 1 above, 63.

Chapter 10

Confucianism and Ten Principles

Confucianism can be considered the most representative philosophy of China's value system from the perspective of both historical development and contemporary influence. Indeed, the role of traditional Confucian values still plays a significant part in Chinese daily life and decision-making. The impact of Confucianism is not only pervasive and significant in China but also it is observed in many East Asian countries, in particular, Korea and Japan. These values are so deeply rooted in people's hearts and minds that they often unaware of its influence. It is also true that Confucian ideas inform decision-making[1] and other actions in the workplace. Confucianism, as a "philosophy of practical life,"[2] is intended to shape people's value systems and their behavior for the sake of social harmony. This is similar in spirit to Peter Drucker's concept of a functioning society.

During its long development, Confucianism has consistently undergone changes through three major historical epochs described as classic Confucianism, Neo-Confucianism, and New Confucianism.[3] It has adopted core concepts from other Eastern philosophies – Taoism and Legalism, the writings of Mencius, and religions such as Buddhism – to its principles and frameworks.[4] Today the most well-known and widely accepted Confucian concepts are probably the fundamental "Five Virtues": benevolence (*ren*), righteousness (*yi*), ritual (*li*), wisdom (*zhi*), and trust (*xin*).[5] These virtues are very much alive today as a "standard of merit" in many Asian countries in both personal and professional life.

Despite its influence and prevalence today, Confucianism is regarded by many people as difficult or impossible to understand. Besides potential misunderstandings caused by dramatic changes in language over time,[6] Confucianism is often seen as complex and difficult to connect to modern life. Nevertheless, we have observed an increasing interest in this topic, especially in regard to three questions: Are traditional cultural values still applicable today? Does Confucianism impact management practices in Confucian societies? Is Confucianism compatible with Western management theories that are practiced today?

Creating the Organization of the Future, 123–152
Emerald Publishing Limited, Howard House, Wagon Lane, Bingley BD16 1WA, UK.
First published as 当德鲁克遇见孔夫子 (*"Setting the Direction for Your Firm"*) by Orient Publishing Center ("OPC"), with Bernard Jaworski and Virginia Cheung, China, 2021. English language translation copyright © 2023, Emerald Publishing Limited. This English language edition published under exclusive licence from OPC by Emerald Publishing Limited. Translated by Bernard Jaworski and Virginia Cheung. The moral right of the copyright holder and translator has been asserted.
All rights of reproduction in any form reserved
doi:10.1108/978-1-83753-216-220231010

Most existing studies on the application of Confucianism to modern management are limited to the area of business ethics. As such, the literature lacks a systematic framework for applying Confucianism to the broader field of management. However, we argue that, as a pragmatic philosophy[7] that has directed everyday life in Ancient China for thousands of years, Confucian principles can be applied to business settings and inspire modern general management thinking and practice. This is especially true in Confucian societies like China.

To effectively grasp and apply Confucian principles, various perspectives must be understood. Considering that most organizations in China today adopt management theories that are aligned with Western values, we need to summarize and articulate the core principles in a practical, managerially-friendly way to make it clear how this ancient philosophy works within a contemporary, cross-cultural setting. This is why, like in Chapter 9, we have summarized 10 representative general principles drawn from the works of several widely recognized Western Confucian scholars. Moreover, we have added new meaning and explanations to reflect contextual changes to these principles over time. Finally, we have expanded these ideas into the context of contemporary business to better illustrate how today's management professionals can continue to benefit from these principles.

Ten Principles

Virtuous and Ethical Behavior Creates a Harmonious Society

Similar to Drucker's heavy emphasis upon the human element in management, Confucianism is also a human-centered philosophy. It focuses on the inner self and self-cultivation with the aim of shaping oneself toward "junzi" – to be a "superior person" through continuous reflection, practice, and evaluation. Although this journey is lifelong, Confucius believed that human beings are naturally inclined toward good conduct,[8] so everyone has the chance to become "junzi" through dedicated effort. This aligns with the Drucker principle of "employee orientation." Drucker believed that organizations should invest in the development of everyone – not just "high potentials" or other favored organizational groups.

If each and every individual can behave virtuously and become superior through self-cultivation, then they can continue to lead their families, manage their country, and ultimately serve beyond national boundaries until society as a whole reaches harmony through collective effort.[9] Once again, this approach is consistent with Drucker's four levels of management: managing oneself, managing teams, managing the organization, and, finally, creating a functioning society.

Confucius defines a superior person as "having a sense of appropriate conduct as one's basic disposition, developing it in observing ritual propriety, expressing it with modesty, and consummating it in making good on one's word."[10] Achieving this quality as a person requires that many core virtues work together; this idea of self-cultivation echoes Drucker's well-known view that organizations need values "as a human body needs vitamins and minerals."[11]

Confucius cautioned that the superior person "thinks always of virtue; the common man[12] thinks of comfort,"[13] but achieving this level of self-cultivation is a very difficult task. He used a well-known metaphor that self-cultivation is similar to the way that someone will "polish rough jade into a beautiful statue."[14] In other words, reshaping one's mindset and behavior can be a very time-consuming and arduous process (see Fig. 10.1).

Transferred into an organizational context, self-cultivation can be interpreted as self-growth and self-management. While the importance of growing people has been well-recognized by modern organizations, the reality is that it takes time for an organization to shape a strong culture. Often there is resistance to organizational change. This is because, just as Confucianism recognized, a healthy, harmonious outer environment can foster self-cultivation. By the same token, overall societal advancement can be achieved only when all members practice virtue together. Drucker not only advocated self-management and individual growth but also suggested that organizations carry the responsibility to train and develop their employees just as, in Confucianism, one polishes "rough jade" into "beautiful statue" or, within the Confucian family, the father-son relationship requires the parent to take responsibility for educating his children.

Benevolence, which is "the virtue of all virtues,"[15] is the cornerstone of Confucianism, and it represents an attitude of outward love to all people that is similar to today's altruism. From Confucius's perspective, one who is benevolent should "see as his first priority the hardship of self-cultivation, and only after think about results or rewards,"[16] as described in *Analects*. If organizations can shape such a benevolent culture, the environment will motivate the organization's individuals to advance their moral refinement.

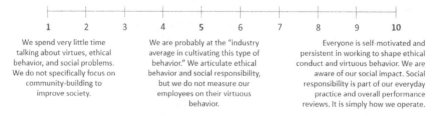

The ultimate goal of Confucian philosophy is a harmonious society. Harmony in society is a result of the virtuous and ethical behavior of individual members. Self-cultivation is achieved by continuous reflection, practice, and evaluation.

1	2	3	4	5	6	7	8	9	10

We spend very little time talking about virtues, ethical behavior, and social problems. We do not specifically focus on community-building to improve society.

We are probably at the "industry average in cultivating this type of behavior." We articulate ethical behavior and social responsibility, but we do not measure our employees on their virtuous behavior.

Everyone is self-motivated and persistent in working to shape ethical conduct and virtuous behavior. We are aware of our social impact. Social responsibility is part of our everyday practice and overall performance reviews. It is simply how we operate.

Fig. 10.1.   Virtuous and Ethical Behavior Creates a Harmonious Society.

But, at the same time, every employee must willingly work on his or her own self-cultivation (i.e., self-development, instead of just waiting for organized training or for someone else to share their benevolence). Confucian scholar Zhu Xi[17] has recognized the difficulty of persisting in the self-cultivation process and suggested that the motivation should come from within.[18] Individuals must have a strong mind and strong self-discipline; it cannot be forced by others: "Looking, listening, speaking, and moving are all things that come from oneself, not from others, which is why the key to achieving Goodness lies within oneself and does not come from others."[19] From Drucker's perspective, everyone within the organization should have the intrinsic motivation to be contribution-driven, responsible, and accountable.

This is not to say we can fully rely on employees' intrinsic motivation and cultural influence; we also need a system that supports self-cultivation. In ancient times, the reward for being value-led could be improving social status and gaining more respect instead of being stuck in a category because of your birth or profession. Entrepreneurs in ancient China had lower social standing than other formally educated scholars (civil servants), but they had an opportunity to improve their social status, gain respect, and be recognized as "Confucian traders."[20] Interestingly, this concept is akin to Drucker followers and Drucker-like enterprises that follow his management philosophy. In today's organizational setting, self-cultivation often translates into movement upward in the organizational ranks.

Confucius advocated that self-cultivation was the responsibility of everyone as members of society, regardless of their social class.[21] Master Yangming[22] argued that social class should not be the reason to stop being virtuous. All occupations, roles, and functions should be virtuous. Today, if we consider an organization as a society in itself, aiming for a harmonious organizational, a strong culture requires a collective effort. All higher-ranked executives or operational staff should be equally virtuous in mind and conduct.

Even when there are managers or coworkers who are not being virtuous, employees shouldn't abandon self-cultivation. Instead, they should continue to cultivate themselves because that intrinsic effort will guide them. "I will have within myself the means to restrain my eyes and not to look at it," Confucius said, "restrain my ears and not to listen to it, restrain my mouth and not to speak of it, and restrain my heart and not to put it into action."[23]

If we think of a harmonious society as the external environment in which an organization operates, each organization has the responsibility to self-cultivate so that it can contribute to society overall. This is akin to the concept of corporate social responsibility involving organizations and individuals pursuing socially responsible activities. The core virtue of righteousness is credited as the "primary driver of corporate social responsibility" in Chinese value systems.[24] In a business setting, this virtue provides the reasoning for why organizations should do what is right in support of the social good.

Along with being socially responsible to work *for* social harmony, this principle also can be interpreted as a harmonious fit between an organization and its external environment. That is, the organization does no harm *to* society in its daily operations such as seeking nonexploitative ways to integrate with nature,[25] reducing destructive competition in the market, refraining from activities that are not environmentally friendly, or minimizing production of undesirable byproducts.[26] These are very similar to Drucker's principle "Demonstrate Social Responsibility." The concept of sustainability and "environmental, social, and governance" (ESG) is emphasized across the globe today, and these are all examples of that harmonious Confucian principle.

All of these examples align with Drucker's principle of demonstrating social responsibility, and they demonstrate how to achieve overall good by promoting self-cultivation on an individual level and on the organizational level so that they fit into society in a harmless way.

Manage by Virtue Rather Than by Punishment

Confucius believed in the "universal existence of moral law."[27] He advocated that it is more effective to rule a country by promoting moral values than by punishment, given that each individual has a natural intrinsic motivation to pursue virtuous activities. Following this principle, organizations should prioritize being virtues-led, balancing the right level of tolerance before punishment, allowing individuals to make mistakes, guiding them to improve, and learning from mistakes.

A commitment to virtues is the prerequisite to lead by virtue. Building on the previous principle that Confucius believed human beings have an innate sense of benevolence and that everyone is teachable, individuals possess a natural tendency to perform virtuously. This assumes individual employees have the willingness to learn values and behave in accordance with what they learn. That is, they not only learn virtues conceptually but also practice them at work (see Fig. 10.2).

This Confucian principle states that promoting virtue is the most effective form of management. Self-cultivation to "do good" should be prioritized over punishment.

1	2	3	4	5	6	7	8	9	10

We have clearly defined rules and we enforce them in our daily managerial practice. We impose rules and regulations as the most effective way to discipline employees who are not performing as expected. Virtue is not our priority.

We promote virtue, but we also use punishment. People don't always choose to do what is right, so we try to balance value promotion and punishment. We punish the "bad" and promote the "good" at the same time.

Our organization is values-led rather than performance-led. Our values and our mission are our polestars. We measure and promote employees by values. We have rules and regulations, but we believe that if employees completely buy into our values, there will rarely be a need to punish or enforce rules.

Fig. 10.2.   Manage by Virtue Rather Than Punishment.

The first step for any organization is to clearly define and articulate its desired values and cultural behavior (code of conduct). Next, organizations must communicate with employees their organizational values and expected behaviors. Everyone must buy into the organizational values – or decide they are not a good fit. Confucius termed this desired virtuous behavior as rituals, and we can understand rituals as today's cultural behavior or organizational practices. Confucian rituals form a model of ethical behavior designed for people to learn and practice in order to shape social norms.

Righteousness, which is another core virtue, can empower employees to recognize what is right and wrong and to make the best choices in a given context. Righteousness is also associated with a sense of shame and disdain.[28] Therefore, on an individual level, righteousness can teach people to feel ashamed of their own misconduct so that they stop without needing to receive any kind of punishment. On an organizational level, righteousness leads to a higher level of tolerance for employee mistakes. As Confucius explained: "If you try to guide the common people with coercive regulations and keep them in line with punishments, the common people will become evasive and will have no sense of shame. If, however, you guide them with virtue, and keep them in line by means of ritual, the people will have a sense of shame and will rectify themselves."[29]

Confucius added that, "One who rules through the power of virtue is analogous to the polestar: it simply remains in its place and receives the homage of the myriad lesser stars."[30] This again emphasizes the importance of making virtuous decisions that are always aligned with the directional polestar. However, requiring today's employees to buy into one unified set of values is complex. In today's diversified society, personal value systems can be dynamic and change in a short period of time.[31] Modern organizational culture theory suggests that the development of personal values can vary depending on an individual's life experience, changes in the external environment,[32] and how the individual views the environment.[33] Thus, today's organization must accommodate diversified personal values as long as they are generally compatible with the overall values of the organization.

To align personal values to organizational values can result in short-term turnover, but this is a helpful two-way process that can keep and attract the "right" talent for the organization. This process can take time, and recognition via awards and promotions can be powerful tools to foster this process. For example, placing values-led individuals in positions of power as role models for others instead of being "performance-led" only or selecting "disciples" to promote shared values to a greater population within the organization. During this hiring and selection process, individuals might find their personal values cannot be aligned with the organizational values, and, if that's the case, they should seek out other organizations that are a better value fit for them.

Many Confucian virtues are general principles rather than explicit rules, and it can be difficult in most cases to relate conceptual values to daily behaviors (except maybe safety regulations or processing). People may find Confucian principles and values too vague to practice, particularly in the face of changing contexts or complex issues.[34] This makes the concept of "ruling by virtue" particularly challenging.

It's interesting that, even though Confucius prioritized virtue over punishment, he didn't completely dismiss the use of force. Rather, he just viewed it as a last resort. In fact, enforcing the rules and regulations is not in conflict with ruling by virtue; modern theories of organizational culture also emphasize the importance of prioritizing values: "Invoking myths and values to create institutional legitimacy created interest in the role culture plays in organizations."[35]

In modern organizations, virtues work similarly to values. As a fundamental component of overall organizational culture, promoting values can guide people's behavior in terms of "how we do things around here."[36] Having compelling organizational values can lead everyday decision-making in the workplace (wisdom),[37] motivate employees toward desired behaviors (ritual) voluntarily rather than by punishing them (righteousness), and direct work priorities.[38] In this way, the organization can shape a loving culture (benevolence) that is values-led with a high level of tolerance. As the organization develops its values and culture, executives and employees can be better motivated to continue self-cultivation in order to promote ruling by virtue.

Do What's Right Rather Than Simply Being Profit-Driven

This is not a principle that is "opposed to profit-making"[39] but merely suggests that people do what is right without calculating profit.[40] This principle provides the reasoning and motivation for today's organizations to make the right choices in their objectives and to consider the overall prosperity of the community rather than just profit maximization. Confucius said, "The superior man, in the world, does not set his mind either for anything, or against anything; what is right he will follow."[41]

It's not shameful for a "superior person" to make profit, but the unvirtuous behavior of pursuing personal gain should be distained. "The Gentleman understands rightness," Confucius said, "whereas the petty person understands profit."[42] At the time when Confucius said this, there was a common misunderstanding that people thought money was menial and should be disdained. Today people have realized it is a misinterpretation, the belief that Confucianism does not encourage profit-making[43] still remained its influence. In fact, the statement that the "petty man understands profit" refers to profit-driven motives and behavior rather than profitability itself. In other words, Confucianism is strongly against profit maximization through unvirtuous behavior, but not against doing business in and of itself (see Fig. 10.3).

The misguided association between profit and "the petty man" has not only negatively affected the social status of entrepreneurs throughout history but also it continues to influence people's mindsets and behavior today. Many people in Confucian societies today are still ashamed to talk about money, either in their private lives or in their business activities. A lack of clear and direct

The Confucian principle of righteousness requires knowledge of what's right and what's wrong. People should choose to do what's right instead of being motivated solely by profit or other considerations.

1	2	3	4	5	6	7	8	9	10

The primary reason for our business to exist is to make money. Our measurements are solely based on financial performance. We translate everything into monetary value. We strive to increase our profit margin by lowering costs, even at the expense of our suppliers and others in the value chain.

We are aware of our social responsibility and values, but we are also profit driven. We try to maintain a balance between the two. We know what's right, but recognize that it's hard to do what's right at all times, especially when potential gain is significant.

Everyone in the organization knows what's right and does right. We create compelling objectives that reflect our values. We are committed to ethical business practices. We do not trade off our values for immoral actions or pursue gain at the expense of others, even when it may be profitable.

Fig. 10.3.   Do What's Right Rather Than Simply Being Profit-Driven.

communication on money can still cause misunderstandings between employees and their employers or between business partners.

Righteousness is often associated with disdain,[44] suggesting that people who knowingly do wrong should be disdained. Like Confucius, Drucker stated that "not knowingly doing harm" should be the basic rule for professional ethics and public responsibility.[45] Making the "right choice" to adhere to virtuous behavior and not prioritize profitability over other goals should come from one's own motivation rather than from external forces. Although material profits can be motivating, Drucker suggested that profit should be the result of value creation and not the primary motivator and sole purpose for a business. For Drucker it was "virtuous" and socially responsible for organizations to make a sufficient profit in order to continuously deliver value. But if a business only seeks to maximize its own profit by raising prices or using lower quality materials to control costs, these behaviors would be considered "unvirtuous" and should be distained according to Confucian principle.

The virtue of righteousness is designed to empower people to make the "right choice," and people should voluntarily not do what is wrong even when they're faced with strong temptation.[46] This applies to both mindset and behavior (i.e., if one's mind is solely profit-driven, even without obvious misconduct and harmful consequence this would already be considered unvirtuous by Confucius).

Confucius's famous statement that "gentlemen do not pursue externalities"[47] does not mean that people must stay poor to be virtuous; rather, making the "right choice" should be rewarded with some kind of material benefit. In ancient China, the family was the basic production unit of the agriculture-based economy, and people were very dependent on each other in their production activities. So, individuals who were able to make socially desirable choices would foster long-term economic activities. But for those who didn't, the entire family of that unvirtuous individual would "lose face" within their community. The impact of this can be seen in economic terms: such a situation could result in harming that family's long-term ability to support itself and make money within a closed economy. So, this principle has a strong pragmatic dimension – it builds both systems of reward and punishment by increasing the cost for those who chose to intentionally do what wasn't socially best. As Confucius noted, "To act with an eye to personal profits will incur a lot of resentment."[48]

Having such information – about right and wrong – is something also necessary to any organization today. Although it is mission impossible to have a completely unified definition of what is considered "right" in today's diverse world, the important point in this Confucian teaching is that the mind simply should be guided by virtuous thinking, not by what is profitable.[49] Similar to Drucker's principle that a successful individual or firm "balances short-term and long-term results," organizations need to trade off short-term gains to pursue their long-term objectives by committing to virtuous practices and values. Thus it's critical that organizations must be able to identify "virtuous" objectives – for example, a compelling mission, vision, and purpose – and apply an ethical practice to their approach so that they generate a profit with integrity.

Confucius raised concerns about the close correlation between profit generation and greed. Today, his perspective is still shared by many people. Today there is an increasing trend to attach "greed" with "profit maximization" as a necessary element in order to have business success, just as Gordon Gecko, the villainous character in Oliver Stone's 1987 movie *Wall Street*, famously said: "Greed is good." Greed can grow and spread very fast, so it is important that an organization treat being virtue-led as an absolute[50] if it wants to be successful in this way. Like Confucius, Mencius explained, "A fully righteous person would also recognize that it is just as shameful to accept a large bribe as it is to accept a small bribe."[51] This focus in Confucianism upon raising people's awareness of a profit-driven mindset was aimed at promoting self-control of greed. Without this awareness, one's sense of mission quickly becomes distorted. At the organizational level, to pursue objectives that result in better financial performance but knowingly harm stakeholders may end up being recognized as business success. In this respect, then, this principle also closely relates to today's concept of self-management.

A Journey of One Thousand Miles Begins With One Step

This principle further demonstrates the pragmatic nature of Confucianism. Confucianism is widely regarded as "close in theories and practice,"[52] and the essence of this principle is to emphasize the importance of action, as we can find implementation being emphasized throughout Confucian works. The statement "the Way is made in the walking of it"[53] suggests that Confucius understood that simply knowing a concept does not produce results: it is the actual action informed by the concept that makes the real difference. As an educator, Confucius himself did not stop at teaching ideas but also encouraged people to act on them (see Fig. 10.4).

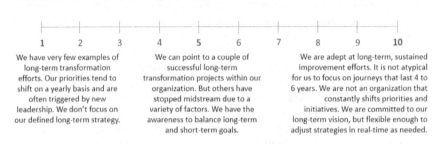

Fig. 10.4.   A Journey of 1,000 Miles Begins With One Step.

Translated into a business context, this principle suggests that organizations must act on their ideas, which relates to Drucker's concept of being results-driven. While Confucius promoted action as the first step in achieving results, he did not explicitly define the exact relationship between activity and results or discuss how the two work together.

Today's organizations often wonder if their employee training efforts will effectively translate into action: Confucius worked with his students in a two-step process. First, he taught them, then he imposed actions, activities, and tasks that would produce a direct result.

In addition to being results-driven, the often-quoted statement that "a journey of one thousand miles beings with one step"[54] reminds us that Confucius wasn't just focused on results; he also emphasized the importance of taking a first step in the whole process. His focus upon the whole process is akin in some ways to what is known today as taking the formative approach. To design an effective process for transformation, small steps and milestones must be clearly defined; it is each of these steps that brings the organization closer to the final result. As Confucius further explained, it is the accumulated actions that make up the process that achieves the ultimate goal. He said, "the Way is long, but with every step one is making progress."[55] The popular metaphor that nearly all Chinese learn at childhood – that "a person who moves a mountain begins by carrying away small stones"[56] – explains that creating lasting change requires a continuous, persistent effort and long-term commitment. "If I stop even one basketful of earth short of completion," Confucius explained, "then I have stopped completely. It might also be compared to the task of leveling ground: even if I have only dumped a single basketful of earth, at least I am moving forward."[57]

In addition to continuous efforts, Confucius also pointed out the importance of goal setting, which decides the direction of your action plan. On an individual level, for example, the journey of self-cultivation must be led by aiming to be that perfectly virtuous superior, not to maximize personal gain. As Master Yangming explained, "If you set your will upon the Way then you will become a scholar of the Way and Virtue, whereas if you set your will upon the cultural arts, you will become merely a technically skilled aesthete. Therefore, you cannot but be careful about the direction of your will. This is why, when it comes to learning, nothing is as important as focusing upon the correct goal."[58] In terms of setting correct directional goals, the creation of a mission, vision, and purpose as we discussed in the first section of this book are fundamental to performance and survival for organizations today. After the organizational direction has been defined, the second step, as this principle states, that each employee must act on that direction in his or her own "Way" to make the material changes in his or her own role.

The well-known term "the Way" presents a road-building process for people "to lead through."[59] It is one's own responsibility – similar to any executive's responsibility in an organization – to present "a Way" that fits their own situation and role within the organization. There is simply no fixed path or best methodology to reach the goal.[60] Just as Drucker advocated that organizations unleash employees' individual potential to make decisions consistent with the organizations mission, driving the process by "making the journey one's own"[61] is very important, too.

Even when everyone in the organization recognizes and shares the same goal, the process of transformation can be long and difficult because human nature takes time to adapt and change. This is why organizations must remain committed to long-term goals while making real-time adjustments in their strategy. As Confucius stated, "When it is obvious that the goals cannot be reached, don't adjust the goals, adjust the action steps." This principle is particularly practical in today's fast-changing VUCA time – that organizations need to be flexible enough to act quickly to changes with persistent and continuous efforts.

Everyone in the Organization Works Toward a Common Goal

Despite the conventional stereotype that Western philosophies focus more on individualism and Eastern philosophies stress collectivism, modern philosophers actually view Confucianism as naturalism, which places the individual in the social context but also emphasizes individual development.[62] Although Confucius's self-cultivation is based on individual efforts to nourish one's own virtue, the aim of self-cultivation is to become superior not just for personal betterment but also to contribute to a harmonious society. A superior individual is further expected to leverage his or her knowledge to better manage family, country, and, ultimately, society overall.[63] This self-development in Confucianism provides different motives than what we normally think about today; self-cultivation itself is designed as a path to reach the shared goal rather than the individual one (see Fig. 10.5).

Thus, in traditional Confucian society, individuals are encouraged to compromise their own self-interest in response to external forces from the family or community, and this is especially true when the commitment to the common

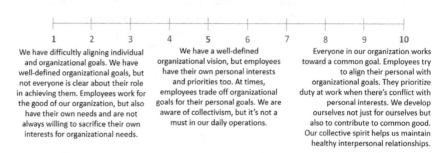

To reach a common goal or vision, everyone in the organization must work together. When there's conflict between the organizational goal and individual goals, organizational goals should be the priority.

1	2	3	4	5	6	7	8	9	10

We have difficultly aligning individual and organizational goals. We have well-defined organizational goals, but not everyone is clear about their role in achieving them. Employees work for the good of our organization, but also have their own needs and are not always willing to sacrifice their own interests for organizational needs.

We have a well-defined organizational vision, but employees have their own personal interests and priorities too. At times, employees trade off organizational goals for their personal goals. We are aware of collectivism, but it's not a must in our daily operations.

Everyone in our organization works toward a common goal. Employees try to align their personal with organizational goals. They prioritize duty at work when there's conflict with personal interests. We develop ourselves not just for ourselves but also to contribute to common good. Our collective spirit helps us maintain healthy interpersonal relationships.

Fig. 10.5.   Everyone in the Organization Works Toward a Common Goal.

good conflicts with an individual's self-interest.[64] This expectation of self-sacrifice is closely related to the concept of harmonious personal interrelationships promoted by Confucianism[65] that are not as common in Western philosophies. Even today, this mindset remains a strong influence in people's decisions and expectations for their career goals in Confucian societies. For example, talented artists or innovative engineers transfer to management roles, simply because it is more in accordance with family or social expectations.

Confucian family values are based on the virtue of benevolence and the concept of selfless love that encourages voluntary contributions like devotion and sacrifice to keep harmony within the family. Shifting from the family to the organization, organizations are widely regarded as extended families in Confucian societies with employee contributions viewed as their obligation to maintain the prosperity of the family. This concept partially aligns with Drucker's teaching that every employee should be contribution-driven.

Confucius requests the same level of devotion, loyalty, and obedience regardless of the situation, whether an individual is promoted or dismissed from the office.[66] Although it may sound unreasonable to require one's willingness to prioritize the common good over one's personal experience, the rationale is simply that every individual balances multiple roles at the same time. Mencius explains that, although duties may vary between family, state, society, and the overall environment we live in, any duty may inevitably require sacrifice.[67] These "sacrifices" represent unavoidable "strategic tradeoffs" we have to make to handle all of these multiple duties. In practice, this can be as simple as employees giving up personal holiday time to prioritize urgent work regardless of the size of their roles; or being promoted, downgraded, or rotated to positions that shouldn't affect employees' willingness to perform.

If we understand this from the perspective of duty transitivity, individuals should naturally share a part of the common duties and treat them as their own duties. It is easier said than done, though, especially for today's knowledge workers and members of Generation Z. Using today's role theory to explain this phenomenon, the roles are simply more "relaxed" in today's diversified organizations. Individuals have much more information and knowledge than they did before to understand of their obligations in relation to general social desirability; they tend to define their own roles.[68] Today's situation is far different from Confucius's time when people had only a few roles and willingly accepted what they were told, which made it easier for people to buy in to a set of shared values and a common goal. But today's social desirability has been reshaped by Drucker's concept of unleashing employees' potential. Executives should not expect employees to work as a collection of spare parts in a machine to be moved around and used according to the organization's need. Indeed, Drucker noted that a firm's focus on human resources needed to emphasize the human element (i.e., a firm hires the whole person) not the resource element (which implies a machine metaphor).

Nevertheless, selfless love and personal sacrifice are not unconditional in orthodox Confucianism. Rather, Confucian teaching promotes mutual responsibility. This means that managers must rule by virtue, take care of employees' interests, and lead by a clearly defined collective mission, vision, and purpose. Further, "sacrifice" should apply to all members equally; it should not be used as a tool for unethical gain by a certain interest group or for office politics. As Confucius clearly stated, he was against "blind loyalty" in the event that managers are not managing effectively for the common good. Likewise, to voluntarily prioritize organizational needs is never an easy task for employees. Today's studies also find it challenging for executives to "love and care" for all employees equally to achieve collective well-being and note that "love is largely absent from most modern corporations."[69] This might explain why Confucius promoted self-cultivation as a perquisite for collective spirit; this applies to both managers and employees.

Given that this Confucian principle can be correctly practiced, everyone who works toward a common goal can support shaping healthy interpersonal relationships within the organization as a way of binding everyone together.[70] In fact, Drucker similarly realized the role of relational contexts in the practice of virtues. He described Confucianism as an "ethic of interdependence, an ethic of mutual obligations."[71] As mentioned previously, this relationship-focused mindset originated in the agriculture-based economy of Confucius's time because collectivism made it easier for people to accept certain personal sacrifices to maintain a harmonious relationship for their long-term benefit. Today, despite rapid urbanization and economic restructuring, a wider connection remains fundamental to the growth of business, and at the same time, people need a sense of belonging within a group. As today's "embedded culture" theory suggests people are entities embedded in a collective team with a shared life, "personal sacrifices" are also identified as "contributions" even though these two concepts are in fact not the same.

Do to Others What You Want Done to Yourself

As stated by Master Yangming: "To manifest the illustrious virtue is to establish the nature of the unity of Heaven, Earth, and all things, to love people is to exercise the function of that unity."[72] Confucian benevolence is a caring tendency that should not be limited to family ties but can be applied to all in need, regardless of whether the relationship is close or far. In an organizational context, this refers to extended care from internal shareholders and employees to the external stakeholders as well as the idea of "establishing others as to establish yourself"[73] which means that you help with others' work in addition to your own duty.

"Do not impose on others what you yourself do not want": This may be the most well-known statement in Confucian teaching. It is often translated as "treat others the way you want to be treated." Compassion and reciprocity form the essential source of this principle and are associated with the virtues of benevolence[74] and understanding,[75] respectively. However, this concept is not unique to Confucian societies: it is mirrored in the "Golden Rule" that exists in other religions and cultures as an "ethic of reciprocity."[76] (See Fig. 10.6).

Compassion requires the ability to put oneself in another's place to show one's care to others. Its primary aim is to promote the sense of consideration from a positive perspective of benevolence. But Confucius also emphasized the prohibitive form of this trait, which is to teach people not to harm others. We can understand the previous principle – "not to prioritize personal gain at the expense of others" – as one application of this principle.

This teaching applies both individual and organizational levels. If we look at the organizational level, this principle and the virtue of benevolence lead to a deeply-rooted "family culture." This is one of the most preferred organizational cultures in Confucian societies – people viewing organizations as their extended families.

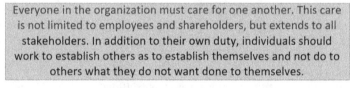

Everyone in the organization must care for one another. This care is not limited to employees and shareholders, but extends to all stakeholders. In addition to their own duty, individuals should work to establish others as to establish themselves and not do to others what they do not want done to themselves.

1	2	3	4	5	6	7	8	9	10

Our employees tend to focus on themselves. They don't share or help each other, either inside or outside the workplace. Our employees view client service work as a task to accomplish rather than a comprehensive philosophy of treating others as they wish to be treated.	We require our employees to be customer centric and to work toward serving the needs of all stakeholders. However, they often don't share their knowledge with each other, and they don't voluntarily help each other to better serve our clients and the community.	Everyone cares for others like family, both inside and outside the organization. We treat customers' and partners' needs as our own needs, and we understand that when they grow, we grow together. We are keen on socially responsible activities. We completely buy into the principle of doing to others as we want done to ourselves.

Fig. 10.6.   Do to Others What You Want Done to Yourself.

It is of course true that, as members of a work family, managers and shareholders shall principally have the responsibility to support employees. In turn, employees shall understand what their performance is supposed to be – something that Confucius termed as "establishment" and that depends on the overall performance of the organization. In reality, as we all know, it is challenging to pursue perfect benevolence and compassion in most parts of life, personal or professional. Despite Confucius's belief that it is essential to human nature to take care of others within one's family, he also recognized people's natural tendency to prioritize their own responsibilities over those of others.

As a matter of fact, maybe there are only a limited number of people in management who fulfill Confucius's definition of a "superior person" and can truly "establish others as to establish yourself."[77] As Confucius noted, "benevolent persons" establish others in seeking to establish themselves and promote others in seeking to get there themselves."[78] Helping others may incur short-term personal sacrifices, but the "investment" in helping others today will yield a "return" when one needs help in the future. This is akin to the concept of "giving to receive."

This means that managers who want to grow "family culture" must grow both their employees and themselves. When employees perform their duties, the team delivers results together. As Drucker noted: A key responsibility of managers to support their employees' personal growth. From Confucius to Drucker, one effective way to "establish" others' long-term development is to give them knowledge to enable them to have ownership and responsibility over the results of their work. As Confucius explained with a metaphor: "Give a bowl of rice to a man and you will feed him for a day. Teach him how to grow his own rice and you will save his life." This teaching resonates in the era of "knowledge workers" that Drucker predicted.

Further, this principle requires an organization to extend this caring relationship from "family members" to all "nonfamily members," and this wider array of stakeholders includes customers, suppliers, partners, government agencies, the general public, and others. This suggests that the organization should take compassion and reciprocity as guiding principles and treat all of these stakeholders with the same level of love, respect, and consideration that they demonstrate internally. By working with your suppliers and partners to build up a healthy "ecosystem," you are encouraging social responsibility.

Although there was no concept of customers in Confucius's time, if we apply this principle to customers, it is consistent with today's concept of customer orientation. The virtue of compassion encourages employees to put themselves in the shoes of customers and to think what they think, discover what they need, and to do what they want to do – that is, what Drucker emphasized as "value creation to customers."

We might think it would be easier to be benevolent to internal employees than to external stakeholders. But it is interesting that, in some of our empirical work, when organizations in Confucian societies were asked to scale themselves on this principle, it was not unusual to hear that people find it easier to demonstrate care and compassion to external customers than to internal coworkers. This might partially reflect why Haidilao – a popular Chinese restaurant brand among young consumers – prioritizes happy employees over satisfied customers in its statement: "Employees are more important than customers,"[79] although the two go hand in hand because happy employees often create satisfied customers.

"Do to others what you want done to yourself" also applies at a larger scale to society. Today's organizations have an increasing awareness of the social impact incurred by their own daily commercial operations, and they are more willing to contribute through generous sharing. This aspect of social responsibility resonates in modern society through philanthropic activities that fit with each organization's own needs and resources.

We realize it is challenging in today's world to apply this concept of complete selflessness in such a broad way, and there are many realistic limitations to practicing benevolence to a full extent at the organizational level. Even Drucker advised that organizations should not perform social responsibility beyond their limits. This principle, though, depicts an essential quality of the human spirit in an idealized situation; in the real world, individuals and organizations can try to pursue this as much as possible. The directive to "treat others how you wish to be treated yourself" has practical meaning for helping us to build a healthy corporate culture that ultimately benefits all.

Embrace Constant Change

Confucius based his teachings on the notion that "the only constant is change itself."[80] In his view everything changes in all respects in life, from nature to society, and changes can happen at all levels, at all times, and in all institutions, families, and individuals.[81] In Confucianism, change is viewed as natural and desirable as "a great current."[82] Take the example of Way (which refers to the "totality of all things"): It is a dynamic concept from Confucius's viewpoint. He used flowing waters that "never cease day or night" as a metaphor for the constant, changing nature of life.[83]

Although everything changes, Confucian philosophy places more emphasis on the inner self than on external "things" compared with Western philosophies. Change, therefore, can happen not only with "objects" and "things" but also in human beings. Unlike many Western thinkers, who take the view that a human being is "the same person throughout time," Confucius saw people as "changing and growing" all of the time, noting that self-cultivation and changing relationships with others could reshape one into a "different person."[84] As people grow their virtues through self-cultivation – that is "self-development" – people are expected to reshape not only their minds, attitudes, and beliefs but also their behavior and conduct to stay effective. Similarly, organizations must also have flexible strategies in place to reshape their core competency to stay effective and competitive in the marketplace (see Fig. 10.7).

Continued investment in new knowledge is also related to the virtue of wisdom that is gained from reflection and practice. In fact, as noted in *Analects*, the *Book of Changes*[85] was endorsed by Confucius as a source of wisdom,[86] and its concept

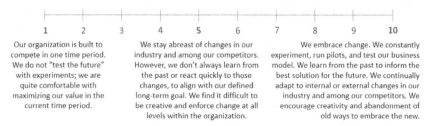

Confucian philosophy is based on the idea that "change is constant" in all institutions, families, and individuals. Effective organizations must embrace change.

1	2	3	4	5	6	7	8	9	10

Our organization is built to compete in one time period. We do not "test the future" with experiments; we are quite comfortable with maximizing our value in the current time period.

We stay abreast of changes in our industry and among our competitors. However, we don't always learn from the past or react quickly to those changes, to align with our defined long-term goal. We find it difficult to be creative and enforce change at all levels within the organization.

We embrace change. We constantly experiment, run pilots, and test our business model. We learn from the past to inform the best solution for the future. We continually adapt to internal or external changes in our industry and among our competitors. We encourage creativity and abandonment of old ways to embrace the new.

Fig. 10.7.   Embrace Constant Change.

of change certainly influenced Confucian thinking.[87] The Confucian concept of constant change has similarity to Drucker's approach that organizations must be vigilant and responsive to outside change. However, Confucius's attitude to change highly relates to the reflection that an organization's growth strategy should reflect the unique adaptations by which organizations become what they are today. The statement "I transmit rather than innovate. I trust in and love the ancient way"[88] was highly criticized as evidence of Confucius being rigidly rooted to the past. However, this should be interpreted as meaning that he encouraged people to learn from history so that ignorance of the past will not limit their future growth. He wasn't being resistant to change. In fact, he said that the most effective individual is someone who is "both keeping past teaching alive and understanding the present – someone able to do this is worthy of being a teacher."[89]

However, the goal is to learn from the past, not stay in it. This learning, he explained, is attained in three ways: "[F]irst, by reflection, which is noblest; second, by imitation, which is easiest; and third by experience, which is the bitterest."[90] This principle has its strong practical meaning today as we see more and more organizations recognizing the importance of learning from reflection and focusing on identifying the "best fit" to create the future, instead of relying on unsustainable imitation or past "successful experience." This idea works similarly to the concept of "no fixed Way" that we briefly touched on in the previous principle, which refers to finding out one's own answer in response to change. In fact, Confucius demonstrated this in his own teachings. As recorded by his students, he gave numerous and different answers to the same question, and this sometimes puzzled even his own disciples.[91] This is because Confucius took context into consideration to provide a customized solution to each of his students. This phenomenon stems from the belief in Chinese tradition that there is no single truth to "look at things" and to "describe events."[92] As Confucius encouraged his students to do their own analysis, organizations that want to lead in a new environment must acknowledge that, even confronted with the same situation, there may be several different solutions and new answers: that is why employees should be encouraged to look for diverse answers and innovative approaches rather than repeating the same practices.

Like Confucius's teachings on change, Drucker also suggested that innovation and abandonment are powerful tools against the uncertainties brought on by change and offer a better way to prepare an organization for enhanced long-term sustainability. Despite Confucius's advocacy of embracing constant change, we also recognize that critics have long questioned Confucius's insistence on rigidly adhering to past rituals.[93] The well-known statement about "look[ing] into [the] past" has been interpreted as more evidence of Confucius being stubborn and resistant to change and abandonment. As mentioned before, the rationale behind this statement is to identify what has changed so that organizations won't rely solely on past experience or past strategies because these no longer apply in today's context. It's worth noting that Confucius actually encouraged abandonment. "When you have faults," he said, "do not fear to abandon them."[94] Confucius recognized that people need to practice abandonment in order to embrace something new. Today that refers to continuously justifying one's viewpoint and knowledge in response to external changes as discussed in regards to the previous Drucker principle.

This may also be the reason why Confucianism is viewed as "revivalism rather than traditionalism or conservatism" in the eyes of Western Confucian scholars like Bryan W. Van Norden, whose position contrasts with the modern Chinese view that Confucianism signifies what is traditional and old. Van Norden thinks that Confucius required people to look at the past and learn from classic texts because he wished for them to revitalize by "rediscovering the deep meaning of the texts, practices, and values of the past" to infuse "positive social changes."[95] Indeed, if we understand Confucius's attitude in his particular historical context, we can see that the constant wars he experienced throughout his life affected his ideology and his willingness to restore a flourishing, peaceful world in which everyone could be virtuous and follow ritual. As recorded in *Analects*, he lamented to his students about the world's imperfection in this way: "If the Way were prevailed in the world, then I wouldn't need to change it."[96] It's clear from this example that Confucius not only recognized change but also wished for more positive and value-led social change[97] because we cannot be ignorant of the past if we want a better future and more growth.

Just as the application of Confucian principles requires context and reinterpretation,[98] change in Confucianism is not absolute but must be considered in the context of how it is correlated to other things. As Roger Ames, one of the most respected Confucian scholars, has noted: "Confucius, same as many early Chinese thinkers, never seems to have perceived any substances that remained the same through time... they saw 'things' relationally, and related differently, at different periods of time."[99] Considering the flourish of interrelationship (*guanxi*) culture, Confucian society is indeed a relational-focused society and human relations play an important part in daily decision-making.[100] That said, people must always consider their roles and relationship in the community to decide how to interact with others to perform rituals.[101] By the same token, no organization (family) stands alone in our fast-changing world with increasing relational changes between stakeholders within the ecosystem. Suppliers can become unexpected rivals, and business partners from unrelated industries may become customers: this is why organizations need to think and rethink their positions in the market from a relational-focused perspective. This involves considering all forces and all players in the market that could affect the organization's operations in relation to other market players.

Change can also involve a change in roles but not in one's relationships. As children grow up, for example, their roles will change from being a dependent or beneficiary of their parents to a benefactor on behalf of their parents. In this process, although the supporting behavior and filial relationship are unchanged, the role of children and the direction of the contribution change relative to their parents throughout life.[102] Considering this in an organizational context, a marketing team often relies on a sales team as a window on the market that provides accurate firsthand data about what is changing in the marketplace. But the marketing team also has the role to "repay" the sales team by contributing to this situation by producing analyzed insights that have been generated from the raw data. By the same token, this also applies to the relationship between employees and organization. Employees are both a cost and a resource. This is the "regularities and continuities underlying change" that one finds in Confucianism.[103]

Although Confucius didn't discuss the concept of innovation in response to change, he did demonstrate a creative spirit by giving people the flexibility to practice rituals in alternative ways as long as they stayed within the boundary of their "ritualized roles."[104] To some, this may only mean allowing various options from today's viewpoint, which is not exactly the same as the concept of innovation and customized solution in modern management theories. However, this highlights the importance of creativity in his thoughts according to a postmodern interpretation of Confucianism.[105] Van Norden has recognized Confucius's emphasis on individual creativity as being "reminiscent of Nietzsche or Ralph Waldo Emerson."[106]

Everyone Leads Through Continuous Practice and Reflection

Confucius viewed knowledge as a basic need in life.[107] He was the first to promote the "nobility of virtue" instead of "nobility of blood" to motivate people to pursue education and knowledge. Although Confucius believed that all human beings are fundamentally good, it is each person's ability to continuously learn that determines how an individual grows. "By nature people are similar," Confucius noted, "they diverge as the result of practice."[108]

For Confucius, an effective learning process requires both practice and reflection. Interestingly, although many consider Confucian teaching too vague to apply in real life, for Western Confucian scholars, the teachings are regarded more as "practical know-how" than as "abstract theoretical knowledge"[109] and what these scholars emphasize is how knowledge and action need to be united to obtain the desired results. For them knowledge can only be "absorbed" when people practice it (See Fig. 10.8).

Regarding the importance of reflection to "learning from the past" (which was discussed earlier), Confucius went even further and taught that people could use reflection to learn about anything and everything in life. Everyone makes mistakes. Thus, continuous reflection can help us realize what needs to be rectified. In fact, Confucius admitted that he could be wrong in his own judgments about others,[110] but he could then learn by reflecting on his own failings.[111] "To make a mistake and yet to not change your ways," he said, "this is what is called truly making a mistake."[112]

Although the knowledge available in our fast-changing information age would have been unimaginable in Confucius's time, today's organizations can still leverage from this Confucian learning process to create a unique learning culture by promoting continuous learning, practice, and reflection.

Confucianism has had a significant impact on the modern education system in China. Many teaching methods used there today are based on Confucianism. For example, Confucius wanted people to learn how to learn in addition to studying classic texts. Further, he noted that effective learning requires an open mind: "To know what you know and what you do not know, that is true knowledge."[113] He reminded us not to be judgmental when we learn[114] because everyone can teach us something regardless of their social status and wealth, and we can learn from both of their good and bad actions.[115] Instead of criticizing others, Confucius suggested, we should focus on continuous reflection and improve ourselves by studying the experiences of others to help us with our own self-development.[116]

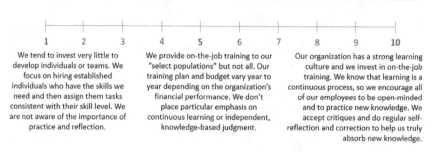

Confucius believed that everyone is educatable. Everyone can—and should—learn to be wise, regardless of their social status and wealth. Learning is a process of self-improvement. Continuous practice and reflection are required to gain wisdom.

1 2 3	4 5 6 7	8 9 10
We tend to invest very little to develop individuals or teams. We focus on hiring established individuals who have the skills we need and then assign them tasks consistent with their skill level. We are not aware of the importance of practice and reflection.	We provide on-the-job training to our "select populations" but not all. Our training plan and budget vary year to year depending on the organization's financial performance. We don't place particular emphasis on continuous learning or independent, knowledge-based judgment.	Our organization has a strong learning culture and we invest in on-the-job training. We know that learning is a continuous process, so we encourage all of our employees to be open-minded and to practice new knowledge. We accept critiques and do regular self-reflection and correction to help us truly absorb new knowledge.

Fig. 10.8.   Everyone Leads Through Continuous Practice and Reflection.

Confucius's focus on learning from reflection is no easy task. "I have yet to meet someone," he said, "who is able to perceive his own faults and then take himself to task inwardly."[117] This is because reflection must be repeated and ongoing. As stated in *Analects:* "[I] constantly examine myself three times a day to keep the integrity long-lasting."[118] This is similar to the practice of organizations that spend a large amount of time, resources, and persistent effort to grow employees. To persist, one must use repeated practice, and this requires a strong mind and motivation.

Confucius also raised the importance of having a healthy external environment in order to create a culture of learning. He suggested that, at the individual level, one can intentionally reduce the "negative external influence [that arises] from the inner sense of eyes and mouth" during reflection to create a heathier environment that nurtures virtuous habits. This is because although Confucius believed each of us has innate goodness from birth, we cannot ignore the "dark side" of our inner hearts and minds. Therefore, regular reflection is the technique that Confucius suggested for mastering the "evil" desires raised in the course of our daily lives (either internally or externally).

It is remarkable that Confucius proposed this concept of continuous learning in his lifetime. In his world, which was based on an ancient agricultural economy, people normally had only one job throughout their lives and learned one skill that would never become obsolete. Tradition was valued much more than innovation. Today there are many organizations that have a sense of urgency when it comes to knowledge and learning because knowledge becomes obsolete so quickly, and they have to adapt their learning culture to stay competitive even though it may take "too much" time and resources. This principle is a reminder that organizations and individual employees must persist in their efforts and "investments" in learning through reflection.

Despite the fact that in Ancient China Confucian works were the only official text to study as a source of wisdom, Confucius also emphasized the importance of critical thinking in effective learning even when studying authoritative works: "It would be better not to have the Documents[119] than to believe everything in them."[120] In an organizational setting, this idea suggests that a learning culture should be able to accept critique, independent thinking, and different opinions from every employee.

As much as Drucker's teaching on innovation needs to be evidence-based, Confucius also noted that innovation should be based on learning and knowledge: "No doubt there are those who try to innovate without acquiring knowledge, but this is a fault that I do not possess. I listen widely, and then pick out that which is excellent in order to follow it; I see many things, and then remember them. This constitutes a second-best sort of knowledge."[121]

These learning methods are consistent with well-established modern organizational practices such as one finds at IBM. To foster innovation and collaboration, for example, an IBM team conducting research on innovative chip structure asked its team members to use different color codes in email.[122] They used white to indicate a fact and to ensure it was evidence-based; green was used to indicate a personal opinion and to promote critical thinking and various viewpoints; and red was used for anything connected with emotion in order to prevent the influence of unnecessary personal negative emotions (which recalls Confucius's reference to "the dark side" of human personalities).

Everyone Follows One Set of Standards and Norms for Behavior

Confucian rituals are regarded as "practicing tools" designed for people to follow according to their own social roles. Today, there are significant critics of orthodox Confucian rituals who view them as obsolete. For twenty-first century organizations, there's no need to follow those ancient ritual practices even though in essence they share many of the same values and codes of conduct that one finds in today's concept of "organizational rituals." From this perspective, this principle is rather consistent with modern organization theory that every organization has "certain values, norms, rules, and beliefs" according to social desirability, and everyone shall "behave in a certain manner according to their particular roles."[123]

Confucian rituals operate on a behavioral level that can take various forms, big or small. In an organization, for example, this can be understood in terms of formal rules and regulations such as processing procedures or accounting standards that have a fundamental impact on business operations. These are rules that must have buy-in from every individual employee and that must be strictly followed in daily operations. There can also be other organizational rituals that are more casual and that function as part of organizational culture (i.e., "how we work here"). From Confucius's perspective, using ritual norms is to be encouraged as benevolent behavior because it demonstrates one's care and awareness of others. If we take following safety requirements as a form of these rituals, this behavior demonstrates each employee's responsibility and accountability to all stakeholders, ranging from coworkers to customers to the organization as a whole (see Fig. 10.9).

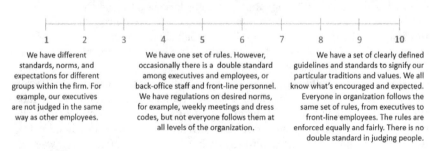

Organizations should have one set of standard, unified social norms for all. Confucianism encourages everyone to behave in accordance with social desirability, with mutual respect and consideration of others.

1	2	3	4	5	6	7	8	9	10

We have different standards, norms, and expectations for different groups within the firm. For example, our executives are not judged in the same way as other employees.	We have one set of rules. However, occasionally there is a double standard among executives and employees, or back-office staff and front-line personnel. We have regulations on desired norms, for example, weekly meetings and dress codes, but not everyone follows them at all levels of the organization.	We have a set of clearly defined guidelines and standards to signify our particular traditions and values. We all know what's encouraged and expected. Everyone in organization follows the same set of rules, from executives to front-line employees. The rules are enforced equally and fairly. There is no double standard in judging people.

Fig. 10.9.   Everyone Follows One Set of Standards and Norms for Behavior.

Regardless of what size and shape these actions take, the key is that rituals must be learned and repeated on a regular basis. As Confucius noted, rules must be practiced until they become incorporated into daily life as habits, and continuous practice itself is a self-cultivation process that is supported by the virtue of wisdom.

The goal of this principle is to encourage and strengthen the collective social order through individual propriety. Even though ritual behavior is practiced on an individual level, it has a communal and organizational dimension when it is accepted as the responsibility of everyone. Think again of the example of following safety guidelines in a company. This clearly has a communal dimension and benefit that depends on every individual following the rules. In fact, standardization was fundamental to business success during the industrialization era, and today this approach remains powerful as a way of enhancing effectiveness in production and managerial practices especially for larger organizations.

For Confucius, the virtue of ritual is "universally applicable to every man."[124] This means that all rituals (rules) are enforced equally and fairly with no double standard allowed. Everyone is judged on the same merits, and there is one standard for everyone, from executives to front-line employees. This effort can further enhance trust within the organization and better connect individuals and groups in a smoother relationship. There is a challenge, though, in organizations dominated by knowledge workers and members of Generation Z because of their ideological distances. In this case, imposing one set of rules and regulations will remain an ongoing issue. In particular, when employees do not realize the importance of standardization, they may view the value of organizational rituals in symbolic terms instead of in terms of substance. This mindset makes enforcing one fixed set of values and a single code of conduct very difficult. Therefore, for individual employees to buy into an organization's standards, organizations should pay attention, clearly define their rules, and communicate to everyone repeatedly (just as Confucius similarly said that rituals must be learned).

In practice, although it's challenging for everyone to buy in to an organization's rules, and these protocols may not be performed perfectly to achieve intended outcomes, having such rituals can play a significant symbolic role as well as acting as internal glue.[125] As organizational culture theory suggests, ritual "fosters belief in the organization's purposes, and cultivates hope and faith."[126] Indeed, rituals can signify particular organizational traditions and values. When everyone on the team follows the same set of rules, the "powerful symbolic pressure" it creates can separate this group of people from others who will be seen as outsiders. This environment creates an atmosphere of "how we work here" and gives employees a sense of ownership as well as embracing new employees in this "communal membership."[127] From this perspective, performing rituals can be a powerful tool to help organizations shape their desired culture[128] through their symbolic and cohesive effects.

Today's organizational theory also suggests that communal rituals as shared values, rules, and laws can reflect a common social demand and desirability.[129] We can also understand Confucian rituals if we treat them in the modern context of "organization as theater," which suggests that organizations have a certain theatrical aspect in the sense that everyone follows "approved dress codes and plays the game by acceptable roles of conduct" according to social desirability.[130] From this perspective, individual employees in an organization must follow these rituals as they apply to their roles within the team.

Never Promise What You Cannot Deliver

This principle is related to the Confucian virtue of trust, which can be understood today in terms of the idea of credibility. Trust in Confucianism is critical to connecting people and creating partnerships to maintain a harmonious society. Trust still matters today and is heavily emphasized in daily conduct both in life and work. This principle offers some practical suggestions for managers so that they can earn the trust of others and maintain a lasting reciprocal relationship with stakeholders (See Fig. 10.10).

Confucius believed that long-lasting relationships were based on reciprocity.[131] In his time, faithfulness was the foundation of the alliances that independent states formed to survive frequent war and conflict. In kinship-based societies, trust naturally stemmed from blood ties within families, but it was different outside of family circles. Building connections with strangers in order to create business partnerships involved higher risks and cost. So merchants had to rely on word of mouth to make their business decisions, and this meant that faithfulness and trustworthiness were the most important character traits that anyone could have.

According to modern management theory, a public awareness of one's best traits and qualities is known as brand recognition and can refer to one's personal brand on the individual level or a corporate brand on the organizational level. A trustworthy brand is still a *sine qua non* in business decisions, and that means that

To develop a harmonious partnership, everyone involved must do what they say they will do. Everyone must be committed to their word at all times, and never overpromise on what they can deliver. Executives should be role models who "walk the talk" to gain trust of their peers and employees.

1	2	3	4	5	6	7	8	9	10
Our organization communicates to stakeholders through branding and marketing, but we cannot always keep our promise to be truly client centric. Internally, we tend to evaluate ourselves by what we say rather than what we do. Our executives sometimes overpromise on staff benefits and promotion opportunities.			We have a solid brand that is trusted by our shareholders and stakeholders. Overall, we do a very good job of delivering what we say we are going to deliver. That said, there is certainly room for improvement. Our executives and managers are exemplars to follow most of the time.			We are reputable because of our trustworthiness with our employees, customers, and partners. We consistently deliver on our product and service quality, as well as our values and social responsibilities, even when they increase our costs or negatively affect our short-term financial performance. Our executives are qualified role models. We work hard to be the most trusted, reliable brand for our clients in the long-term.			

Fig. 10.10.   Never Promise What You Cannot Deliver.

building reliable partnerships with stakeholders and keeping the value of the brand should be prioritized over any short-term gains. As Confucian faithfulness requires people to prioritize virtue over monetary gain at all times, one should principally remain committed to an established contract, partnership, or promise even if doing so may result in short-term loss. When all parties know there is an obvious mutual benefit, for example, it will be easier to keep their word and maintain trust. But if a better deal comes along after a contract has been signed or changes in the market make the partnership seem less attractive, it may become increasingly difficult to stay committed to the partnership even though that is the proper course to take. On the other hand, Confucius did not suggest that it is necessary to build a lasting partnership even at the expense of either party; rather, his teachings suggest that one makes a strategic trade-off by giving up short-term gains to maintain one's credibility and hopefully realize long-term gains. In business practice, this is similar to Drucker's teaching about balancing long-term and short-term goals (balancing short-term economic loss with a long-term gain in trust).

In business, trust is built on action, not words. Confucius noted that "the Gentleman is ashamed to have his words exceed his actions."[132] The fact is, many people talk about virtue, but few can actually put it into daily practice in an organization.[133] Compared to mindset, behavior is more obvious and measurable, and putting it into practice is easier for most to understand. Confucius explained how he leveraged behavior as "KPI" we use today in the area of a personal evaluation assessment: "At first, when evaluating people, I would listen to their words and then simply trust that the corresponding conduct would follow. Now when I evaluate people, I listen to their words but then closely observe their conduct."[134]

There is a clear connection between Drucker's approach and the Confucian concept that "trustworthiness should be judged by actions." Human Resources could leverage this principle and reflect on what explicit behaviors are associated with producing a direct result and how these behaviors can be measured to determine whether or not an individual employee or a team is "trustworthy" in delivering promised goals and objectives.

Confucius further reminded us that having a "clever tongue"[135] is not enough; instead, a superior individual should be "reticent"[136] and promise only what they can deliver[137] and deliver what has been promised.[138]

Building up a high level of trust should be emphasized not only within the organization but also with all stakeholders. For example, the most fundamental behavior that organizations can follow in order to gain trust from their customers is to deliver quality products and promised services. If the organization's long-term suppliers suffer an unexpected soaring energy cost, an excellent example of building trust would involve having the organization share the extra cost with the customers. They would shoulder the short-term difficulties together. From a broader societal point of view, if an organization wants the public to see it as a trustworthy brand, that organization needs to be persistent in its socially responsible efforts. Such efforts are not easy, but as today's study shows, these efforts can create real values that will enhance performance. Among the best performing marketing teams globally, there's always a high level of trust and confidence.[139] Peter Markey, the former CMO of British Post, once confirmed this reciprocal relationship by saying that "shaping a tribe culture that is based on trust and confidence, self-motivation and intelligence can strongly support the success of marketing professionals."[140]

For managers in today's organizations, being a virtuous role model is still an effective way to gain the trust and loyalty of employees. As noted in *Analects:* "One can rule others only after they have purified their own hearts, learned to treat others consistently, and regulated their trustworthiness by means of models and regulations, so that their trustworthiness is clear for all to see. For the model set by the action of their superiors is what the common people will turn to."[141] In fact, Confucius's disciples recorded many instances in which Confucius himself demonstrated model behavior through his teaching.[142] Master Yangming also commented on the power of the role model effect: "Theoretical teaching is certainly useful for teaching one how to act, but it cannot match the sort of profound effect that one can achieve through teaching by example."[143]

Today's employees care about fair and equal treatment, and executives must ensure that they have met all the requirements that they are imposing on their employees. In our empirical study of Chinese organizations, we found that executives who serve as role models who "walk the talk" not only gain trust from their peers and employees but also significantly motivate team members to be more dedicated to their work. Managers and organizations can practice this principle to create smooth and healthy employee relationships that are shaped by a trust-based culture.

Notes

1. Jia Wang, Greg G. Wang, Wendy E. A. Ruona, and Jay W. Rojewski, "Confucian Values and the Implications for International HRD," *Human Resource Development International* 8, no. 3 (2005): 311–326. doi:10.1080/13678860500143285.

2. Poola Tirupati Raju, *Introduction to Comparative Philosophy* (Lincoln: University of Nebraska Press, 1962), 103.

3. Three major historical epochs during Confucianism's development are: classic Confucianism (before the Han dynasty), Neo-Confucianism (developed in the Song-Ming dynasty), and New Confucianism (developed since the twentieth century).

4. Thomas A. Wilson, "Genealogy and History in Neo-Confucian Sectarian Uses of the Confucian Past," *Modern China* 20, no. 1 (January 1994): 3–33. doi:10.1177/009770049402000101.

5. In addition to the Five Constants, other important virtues include loyalty (*zhong*), filial piety (*xiao*), and continency (*jie*).

6. Classic Confucian works, including *Analects*, were written in classic Chinese, which differs from modern Chinese. Some Confucian terms have multiple English translations that are equally accepted and commonly used in Confucian studies.

7. Yi-Pao Mei, *Motse, the Neglected Rival of Confucius* (London: Arthur Probsthain, 1934), 23–25; Poola Tirupati Raju, *Introduction to Comparative Philosophy* (Lincoln: University of Nebraska Press, 1962), 97.

8. Roger T. Ames and Henry Rosemont, *The Analects of Confucius: A Philosophical Translation* (New York: Ballantine Books, 1999), 15.
9. Lei Wang and Heikki Juslin, "The Impact of Chinese Culture on Corporate Social Responsibility: The Harmony Approach," *Journal of Business Ethics* 88, supp. 3 (December 24, 2009): 433–451, https://doi.org/10.1007/s10551-009-0306-7.
10. See note 8 above, 188; Confucius, *Analects*, 15.18.
11. Peter Drucker, *The Essential Drucker* (New York: HarperBusiness, 2008), 210.
12. This can also be translated as "petty man," which, in contrast to a "superior person," represents all the opposite unvirtuous features.
13. Confucius, *Analects*, 4.16.
14. Bryan Van Norden, *Introduction to Classical Chinese Philosophy* (Indianapolis: Hackett Publishing, UK edition, 2011), 134.
15. See note 9 above.
16. Confucius and Edward Slingerland, *Essential Analects* (Indianapolis: Hackett Publishing, 2006), 69; Confucius, *Analects*, 6.22.
17. Zhu Xi was the founder of the "rationalist school" and an influential Neo-Confucian scholar.
18. Confucius, *Analects*, 12.1, reinterpreted by Zhu Xi. "The decision to stop or move forward lies entirely within me, and is not determined by others."
19. See note 16 above, 104; Confucius, *Analects*, 12.1.
20. See note 9 above; Samiul Hasan, ed., *Corporate Social Responsibility and the Three Sectors in Asia* (New York: Springer, 2017), 22.
21. See note 16 above, 69.
22. Wang Yangming is regarded as one of the founders of the Lu–Wang School of Neo–Confucianism (the School of Mind). He has frequently been an inspiration for critics of the orthodox Cheng–Zhu School – one of the other major wings of Neo–Confucianism not just in China but also in Japan.
23. See note 16 above, 104; Confucius, *Analects*, 12.1.
24. See note 9 above.
25. Neal M. Ashkanasy, Celeste P. M. Wilderom, and Mark F. Peterson, *The Handbook of Organizational Culture and Climate* (Thousand Oaks, CA: Sage Publications, 2000), 420.
26. Ibid.
27. Charles Moore, ed., *Philosophy and Culture, East and West: East-West Philosophy in Practical Perspective* (Honolulu: University of Hawaii Press, 1962), 667.
28. See note 2 above, 116.
29. See note 16 above, 4; Confucius, *Analects*, 2.3; The Great Learning.
30. See note 16 above, 4; Confucius, *Analects*, 2.1.
31. See note 25 above, 442.
32. Ibid.
33. See note 25 above, 39; Seligman and Katz, 1996.
34. Wei-Bin Zhang, *Confucianism and Modernization: Industrialization and Democratization in East Asia* (New York: Palgrave Macmillan, 1999), 37.
35. Mary Jo Hatch, *Organization Theory: Modern, Symbolic, and Postmodern Perspectives* (Oxford: Oxford University Press, 1997), 36.
36. Lee G. Bolman and Terrence E. Deal, *Reframing Organizations: Artistry, Choice, and Leadership* (San Francisco: Jossey-Bass, 1991), 263.

37. Warren H. Schmidt, *Managerial Values in Perspective* (New York: American Management Association, 1983); David J. Fritzsche, "A Model of Decision-Making Incorporating Ethical Values," *Journal of Business Ethics* 10, no. 11 (November 1991): 841–852, https://www.jstor.org/stable/25072223

38. See note 25 above, 442.

39. See note 2 above, 107.

40. See note 27 above, 411.

41. Confucius, *Analects*, 4.10.

42. See note 16 above, 12; Confucius, *Analects*, 4.16.

43. Christopher Adair-Toteff, "Max Weber on Confucianism versus Protestantism," *Max Weber Studies* 14, no. 1 (January 2014): 79–96. doi:10.15543/MWS/2014/1/6.

44. See note 14 above, 149; Mengzi 6A6.

45. The first responsibility of a professional was spelled out clearly about 2,500 years ago in the Hipprocratic oath: *primum non nocere*, "above all, not knowingly to do harm." Peter F. Drucker, *Management: Tasks, Responsibilities, Practices* (New York: Harper & Row, 1973).

46. See note 14 above, 42.

47. See note 16 above, 85.

48. See note 8 above, 91; Confucius, *Analects*, 4.12.

49. See note 16 above, 69; Confucius, *Analects*, 4.16, 14.12.

50. See note 14 above, 84; Mengzi 1A1.

51. Lanlan Lai, Pu Dong, Yeye Liu, and Xiaoying Chen, "On Mencius' Key Philosophical Term: Yi CE Translation in the Perspective of Reception Theory," *Chinese Studies* 7, no. 4 (January 2018): 277–285. doi:10.4236/chnstd.2018.74024.

52. See note 27 above, 79–81.

53. See note 8 above, 33; Zhuangzi 4/2/33.

54. Lao Tse, *Tao Te Ching;* Davis E. Froeber, Sandra S. Haskins, Jeff Wood, and Charles A. Haskins, "American-Chinese Multi-Faith Religious Exchanges: Sino-US Multi-Faith Dialogues Build Bridges to Bilateral Understanding," *Journal of Church and State* 52, no. 1 (winter 2010): 138–154. doi:10.1093/jcs/csq030.

55. Confucius, *Analects*, 9.11.

56. Confucius, *Analects*, 9.19.

57. See note 16 above, 27; Confucius, *Analects*, 9.19.

58. See note 16 above, 84.

59. See note 8 above, 45.

60. See note 8 above, 48–50.

61. See note 8 above, 45.

62. See note 27 above, 437.

63. Zengzi, *The Great Learning*. The Great Learning was one of the "Four Books" in Confucianism and comes from a chapter in the "Book of Rites" which formed one of the "Five Classics". Zengzi is one of Confucius's disciples.

64. See note 14 above, 42; Confucius, *Analects*, 5.19.

65. See note 35 above, 167.

66. Confucius, *Analects*, 5.19.

67. See note 2 above, 114.

68. See note 25 above, 438–441.
69. See note 36 above, 401.
70. See note 8 above, 23.
71. Sherwin Klein, "Drucker as Business Moralist," *Journal of Business Ethics* 28, no. 2 (November 2000): 121–128. doi:10.1023/A:1006222808524.
72. See note 2 above, 154.
73. See note 8 above, 110; Confucius, *Analects*, 6.30.
74. See note 14 above, 91; Mengzi 6A6.
75. See note 16 above, 74; Confucius, *Analects*, 15.24.
76. Antony Flew, ed., *A Dictionary of Philosophy* (London: Pan Books, 1979), 134.
77. See note 73 above.
78. See note 8 above, 110; Confucius, *Analects*, 6.30.
79. "The Legendary Customer Service of Haidilao," https://www.linkedin.com/pulse/chinas-customer-service-legend-haidilao-david-chung-tai-wai
80. *Book of Changes* ("The I Ching") is also called "Zhou Yi." Written in the second century BC, it is thought to be the oldest and most abstruse classic in Chinese history. It reputedly originated with Fu Xi, who is a mythical sovereign being and the first of the three primogenitors of Chinese civilization.
81. See note 8 above, 23.
82. See note 27 above, 166.
83. Confucius, *Analects*, 9.17.
84. See note 8 above, 27.
85. See note 80 above.
86. Julian Shchutskii, *Researches on the I Ching* (Princeton,: Princeton University Press, 1979), 213; Richard J. Smith, *The I Ching: A Biography* (Princeton: Princeton University Press, 2012), 46.
87. Confucius, *Analects*, 13.22, 7.17.
88. See note 16 above, 64; Confucius, *Analects*, 7.1.
89. See note 16 above, 5; Confucius, *Analects*, 2.11.
90. Confucius, *Analects*, 16.9.
91. See note 14 above, 46.
92. See note 8 above, 33.
93. See note 14 above, 256.
94. See note 8 above, 73; Confucius, *Analects*, 1.8; also translated as "where you have erred, do not hesitate to mend your ways."
95. See note 14 above, 23.
96. See note 8 above, 215; Confucius, *Analects*, 18.6.
97. See note 14 above, 99.
98. See note 14 above, 19; See note 16 above, 57.
99. See note 8 above, 26.
100. See note 8 above, 23.
101. See note 8 above, 27.
102. See note 8 above, 24.
103. See note 101 above.
104. Confucius, *Analects*, 9.3.
105. See note 14 above, 255.
106. Ibid.
107. See note 2 above, 108.

108. See note 16 above, 49; Confucius, *Analects*, 17.2.
109. See note 16 above, 1.
110. See note 14 above, 41; Confucius, *Analects*, 2.9, 5.10.
111. See note 14 above, 41; Confucius, *Analects*, 7.3, 7.33, 7.34.
112. See note 16 above, 45; Confucius, *Analects*, 15.30.
113. Confucius, *Analects*, 2.17.
114. See note 14 above, 41.
115. Ibid.
116. See note 14 above, 41; Confucius, *Analects*, 7.22.
117. See note 16 above, 15; Confucius, *Analects*, 5.27.
118. Confucius, *Analects*, 1.4.
119. "Documents" refers to the classic works.
120. See note 14 above, 185; Mencius 7B3.
121. See note 16 above, 21; Confucius, *Analects*, 7.28.
122. Thomas Barta and Patrick Barwise, *The 12 Powers of a Marketing Leader: How to Succeed by Building Customer and Company Value* (McGraw-Hill Education, 2016), 151.
123. See note 35 above, 74.
124. See note 2 above, 132.
125. David M. Boje, John T. Luhman, and Ann L. Cunliffe, "A Dialectic Perspective on the Organization Theater Metaphor," *American Communication Journal* 6, no. 2 (winter 2003): 4, https://www.researchgate.net/publication/244955010_A_Dialectic_Perspective_on_the_Organization_Theatre; Bolman and Deal, *Reframing Organizations*, 300.
126. Ibid.
127. See note 36 above, 256.
128. Ibid.
129. See note 35 above, 75.
130. Erving Goffman, 1959, 1974; Boje, Luhman, and Cunliffe, "Dialectic Perspective," 4; Bolman and Deal, *Reframing Organizations*, 288.
131. Geert Hofstede and Michael Harris Bond, "The Confucius Connection: From Cultural Roots to Economic Growth," *Organizational Dynamics* 16, no. 4 (spring 1988): 5–21. doi:10.1016/0090-2616(88)90009-5.
132. See note 16 above, 42; Confucius, *Analects*, 14.27.
133. See note 16 above, 73.
134. See note 16 above, 14; Confucius, *Analects*, 5.10.
135. Confucius, *Analects*, 1.3.
136. Confucius, *Analects*, 12.3.
137. Confucius, *Analects*, 14.27.
138. See note 14 above, 42.
139. See note 122 above, 138–139.
140. Ibid.
141. See note 16 above, 107; Confucius, *Analects*, 12.18.
142. See note 16 above, 40.
143. See note 16 above, 87–88.

Index

Printed in the USA
CPSIA information can be obtained
at www.ICGtesting.com
JSHW011446140923
48513JS00005B/54